T0055016

Nietzsche: A Very Short Introduction

VERY SHORT INTRODUCTIONS are for anyone wanting a stimulating and accessible way into a new subject. They are written by experts, and have been translated into more than 45 different languages.

The series began in 1995, and now covers a wide variety of topics in every discipline. The VSI library now contains over 500 volumes—a Very Short Introduction to everything from Psychology and Philosophy of Science to American History and Relativity—and continues to grow in every subject area.

Titles in the series include the following:

AFRICAN HISTORY John Parker and
    Richard Rathbone
AMERICAN HISTORY Paul S. Boyer
AMERICAN LEGAL HISTORY
    G. Edward White
AMERICAN POLITICAL PARTIES
    AND ELECTIONS L. Sandy Maisel
AMERICAN POLITICS
    Richard M. Valelly
AMERICAN SLAVERY
    Heather Andrea Williams
ANARCHISM Colin Ward
ANCIENT EGYPT Ian Shaw
ANCIENT GREECE Paul Cartledge
ANCIENT PHILOSOPHY Julia Annas
ANCIENT WARFARE Harry Sidebottom
ANGLICANISM Mark Chapman
THE ANGLO-SAXON AGE John Blair
ANIMAL RIGHTS David DeGrazia
ARCHAEOLOGY Paul Bahn
ARISTOTLE Jonathan Barnes
ART HISTORY Dana Arnold
ART THEORY Cynthia Freeland
ATHEISM Julian Baggini
THE ATMOSPHERE Paul I. Palmer
AUGUSTINE Henry Chadwick
BACTERIA Sebastian G. B. Amyes
BEAUTY Roger Scruton
THE BIBLE John Riches
BLACK HOLES Katherine Blundell
BLOOD Chris Cooper
THE BRAIN Michael O'Shea
THE BRICS Andrew F. Cooper
BRITISH POLITICS Anthony Wright

BUDDHA Michael Carrithers
BUDDHISM Damien Keown
BUDDHIST ETHICS Damien Keown
CAPITALISM James Fulcher
CATHOLICISM Gerald O'Collins
THE CELTS Barry Cunliffe
CHOICE THEORY Michael Allingham
CHRISTIANITY Linda Woodhead
CIRCADIAN RHYTHMS Russell Foster
    and Leon Kreitzman
CITIZENSHIP Richard Bellamy
CLASSICAL MYTHOLOGY
    Helen Morales
CLASSICS Mary Beard and
    John Henderson
CLIMATE CHANGE Mark Maslin
THE COLD WAR Robert McMahon
COMMUNISM Leslie Holmes
CONSCIOUSNESS Susan Blackmore
CONTEMPORARY ART
    Julian Stallabrass
COSMOLOGY Peter Coles
THE CRUSADES Christopher Tyerman
DADA AND SURREALISM
    David Hopkins
DARWIN Jonathan Howard
THE DEAD SEA SCROLLS
    Timothy Lim
DECOLONIZATION Dane Kennedy
DEMOCRACY Bernard Crick
DESIGN John Heskett
DREAMING J. Allan Hobson
DRUGS Les Iversen
THE EARTH Martin Redfern

Michael Tanner

NIETZSCHE

A Very Short Introduction

OXFORD
UNIVERSITY PRESS

Great Clarendon Street, Oxford OX2 6DP

Oxford University Press is a department of the University of Oxford.
It furthers the University's objective of excellence in research, scholarship,
and education by publishing worldwide in

Oxford New York

Auckland Bangkok Buenos Aires Cape Town Chennai
Dar es Salaam Delhi Hong Kong Istanbul Karachi Kolkata
Kuala Lumpur Madrid Melbourne Mexico City Mumbai Nairobi
São Paulo Shanghai Taipei Tokyo Toronto

Oxford is a registered trade mark of Oxford University Press
in the UK and in certain other countries

Published in the United States
by Oxford University Press Inc., New York

© Michael Tanner 1994

The moral rights of the author have been asserted
Database right Oxford University Press (maker)

First published 1987 as an Oxford University Press paperback
Reissued 1996
First published as a Very Short Introduction 2000

All rights reserved. No part of this publication may be reproduced,
stored in a retrieval system, or transmitted, in any form or by any means,
without the prior permission in writing of Oxford University Press,
or as expressly permitted by law, or under terms agreed with the appropriate
reprographics rights organizations. Enquiries concerning reproduction
outside the scope of the above should be sent to the Rights Department,
Oxford University Press, at the address above

You must not circulate this book in any other binding or cover
and you must impose this same condition on any acquirer

British Library Cataloguing in Publication Data
Data available

Library of Congress Cataloging in Publication Data
Data available
ISBN 978-0-19-285414-8

32

Typeset by RefineCatch Ltd, Bungay, Suffolk
Printed and bound by
CPI Group (UK) Ltd, Croydon, CR0 4YY

To my father and in memory of my mother

Contents

Abbreviations

After the first mention or so of a particular book of Nietzsche's, I have referred to it by initials, as listed below. All quotations are followed by the initial for the book they come from, and then section or chapter numbers. This can be rather inconvenient in the case of books with lengthy sections, but it is meant to enable readers to consult whichever edition they have to hand.

A	*The Antichrist*
BGE	*Beyond Good and Evil*
BT	*The Birth of Tragedy*
CW	*The Case of Wagner*
D	*Daybreak*
EH	*Ecce Homo*
GM	*The Genealogy of Morals*
GS	*The Gay Science*
HAH	*Human, All Too Human*
NCW	*Nietzsche Contra Wagner*
TI	*Twilight of the Idols*
TSZ	*Thus Spoke Zarathustra*
UM	*Untimely Meditations*
WP	*The Will to Power*

Chapter 1
The Image of Nietzsche

Friedrich Nietzsche (1844–1900) was a German philosopher, almost wholly neglected during his sane life, which came to an abrupt end early in 1889. 'Nietzsche' is the figure in whose name people of the most astonishingly discrepant and various views have sought to find justification for them. An excellent study (Aschheim, 1992) devoted to his impact within Germany between 1890 and 1990 lists, among those who have found inspiration in his work, 'anarchists, feminists, Nazis, religious cultists, Socialists, Marxists, vegetarians, avant-garde artists, devotees of physical culture, and archconservatives,' and it certainly does not need to stop there. The front cover sports a bookplate from 1900 of Nietzsche wearing a crown of thorns, the back cover one of him naked, with remarkable musculature, posing on an Alp. Almost no German cultural or artistic figure of the last ninety years has not acknowledged his influence, from Thomas Mann to Jung to Heidegger.

The story in 'Anglosaxony', to use the term in the title of one book about him, which traces his influence in the Western English-speaking world (Bridgwater, 1972), is similar. Wave after wave of Nietzscheanism has broken over it, though there have been periods when he was in abeyance, being seen as the inspirer of German militarism, and so to be vilified by the Allies. He was extensively, and most inaccurately, translated into English, or a language strangely connected with it, in the early years of the century. For all its archaizing grotesqueness, or partly because of that, it was the only translation of many of Nietzsche's works for almost fifty years.

Then, when his reputation was at its lowest in England and the United States, Walter Kaufmann, an emigré professor of philosophy at Princeton, began retranslating many of the key works, and launched the enterprise with a book that had, for many years after its first appearance in 1950, a determining influence on the way Nietzsche was viewed (Kaufmann, 1974). Kaufmann presented a philosopher who was a much more traditional thinker than the one who had inspired anarchists, vegetarians, etc. To widespread surprise, and only slightly less widespread agreement, Nietzsche turned out to be a reasonable man, even a rationalist. Kaufmann sought to establish comprehensively his remoteness from the Nazis, from all irrationalist movements that had claimed him as their forebear, and from Romanticism in the arts. It became difficult, on this version, to see what all the fuss had been about. Thus began the academicization of Nietzsche, one philosopher among others, to be compared and contrasted with Spinoza, Kant, Hegel, and other leading names in the Western philosophical tradition. Reassured by the breadth of Kaufmann's learning, American philosophers, and then increasingly English ones, took him as a starting-point for their studies of Nietzsche on objectivity, the nature of truth, his relationship to Greek thought, the nature of the self, and other harmless topics, at any rate as treated in their books and articles.

Meanwhile in Europe Nietzsche, who had never been in disgrace there, became after World War II a continued object of study and appropriation for existentialists, phenomenologists, and then increasingly, during the 1960s and 1970s, a cynosure for critical theorists, post-structuralists, and deconstructionists. When the latter two movements first gained a foothold in the United States, then took the country over, it was Nietzsche who once more was acknowledged as the major source of their inspiration. Some analytical philosophers, too, found that he was not so remote from their interests as they had assumed, and, in that reciprocal motion that is so characteristic of academic life, congratulated him on having had, in embryonic fashion, some of their insights, while at the same time reassuring themselves about those insights by invoking his authority. There is now a flourishing Nietzsche industry, and almost certainly more books appear on him each year than on any other thinker, thanks to the appeal he has for so many disparate schools of thought and anti-thought.

It is idle to pretend that he would have been entirely displeased by this phenomenon. During his lifetime (and unless I specify otherwise, I shall always mean by that the one that finished when he went mad in 1889, eleven years before his death) he was almost completely neglected, and though that did not make him bitter, as hardly anything did, it caused him distress because he believed that he had vital truths to impart to his contemporaries which they were ignoring at a terrible cost – one of his most accurate prophecies. But he would have looked with scorn on almost everything that has been written or done under his aegis, and the successful take-over by the academic world, though it cannot compare in horror with some of the other appropriations he has suffered, would have seemed to him most like a final defeat, because he wanted at all costs not to be assimilated to the world of learning, where everything becomes a matter for discussion and nothing for action.

Before we move into an account of his views, it is worth stopping briefly and pondering what it might be about his work that has proved so attractive to such diverse movements and schools of thought. Only later will a clearer answer emerge. But it seems, as a preliminary explanation, that it is precisely the idiosyncrasies of his manner that are first found refreshing. His books, after the early *The Birth of Tragedy* (1872) and the *Untimely Meditations* (1873–6), are usually composed of short essays, often less than a page long and verging on the aphoristic, though, as we shall see, crucially different from aphorisms as normally composed and appreciated: that is, one- or two-line encapsulations of the nature of human experience, demanding acceptance through their lapidary certainty. The number of subjects discussed is vast, including many that it is surprising to find mentioned by a philosopher – such matters as climate, diet, exercise, and Venice. And often his reflections are in no particular order. That means that he is much easier than most philosophers to dip into, and his frequently expressed loathing of systems means that one can do that with a good conscience. Many of his quasi-aphorisms are radical in content, and though one may gain only a vague impression of what he favours, one will certainly find out a great deal about his dislikes, most often expressed in terms that are both witty and extreme. What he seems to dislike is every aspect of contemporary civilization, most particularly that of the Germans, and for the reader that is bracing. His underlying view that if we don't make a drastically new start we are doomed, since we are living in the wreckage of two thousand and more years of fundamentally mistaken ideas about almost everything that matters – in, as it were, the decadence of what was anyway deadly – offers *carte blanche* to people who fancy the idea of a clean break with their whole cultural inheritance. Nietzsche was under no illusions about the impossibility of such a schism.

Even so, the variety of interpretations of his work, which far from diminishing as the decades pass, seems to be multiplying, though in less apocalyptic forms than previously, needs more explanation. It suggests to the outsider that he must have been exceptionally vague, and probably contradictory. There is something in both those charges. But they seem more impressive and damning than they are if one does not realize and continually keep in mind that, in the sixteen years during which he wrote his mature works, from *BT* onwards, he was developing his views at a rate that has no parallel, and that he rarely went to the bother of signposting his changes of mind.

What he more often did was to try to see his earlier works in a new light, surveying his career in a way that suggests he thought one could not understand his later writings without a knowledge of his previous ones, to see how he had advanced; and thus taking himself to be exemplary of how modern man, immured in the decaying culture of the nineteenth century, might move from acquiescence in it to rebellion and suggestions for radical transformation. In 1886 in particular, when he was on the verge, though he could not have known it, of his last creative phase, he spent a great deal of energy on his previous books, providing new, sometimes harshly critical, introductions to them, and in the case of *The Gay Science* writing a long, new, final book. No doubt this was part of his programme for showing that nothing in one's past should be regretted, that there need be no waste. But many commentators have been led astray by assuming that it gave them licence to treat all his writings as though they had been produced simultaneously.

Another factor that has made for misreadings and shocking distortions is a consequence of the fact that, from 1872 at least but probably before that, Nietzsche must have spent most of his time writing. The tally of published books is impressive enough. But he noted down at least as much as he organized into books, and unfortunately much of this unpublished writing (the *Nachlass*) has survived. It would not be unfortunate if there were a universally accepted methodological principle that what he did not publish should under all circumstances be clearly demarcated from what he did, but almost no one observes that elementary rule. Even those who claim that they will do this usually slip into unattributed quoting from the immense *Nachlass* when it confirms the line that they are taking on him. What makes this a particularly dangerous way of proceeding is that on some central concepts, among which the Will to Power and the Eternal Recurrence are perhaps the most important, his thought remained so undeveloped. Nietzsche was often so sure he had struck philosophical gold that he jotted down very many thoughts, but left them unworked out. This provides a commentator with the possibility of pursuing trains of thought that he is attributing to Nietzsche, unimpeded by definite statements. Some have even taken the view that the 'real' Nietzsche is to be found in the notebooks, the published work being a kind of elaborate – very elaborate – set of concealments. That absurd attitude is taken by Heidegger, who is thus enabled to peddle his own philosophy as deriving from and also critical of Nietzsche.

Like all his other commentators, I shall occasionally quote from the *Nachlass*, but I shall indicate when I am doing that. Nietzsche took great pains over the finished form of what he published, and he was the last person to think that style was an optional extra. Since he was a natural stylist, his jottings make more elegant reading than most philosophers' finished products. But when one compares his published thoughts with his draft versions of them, the difference is striking enough to make anyone cautious of taking them as being on a par, one would have thought. I emphasize this point because, as we shall see, the manipulation of what Nietzsche wrote has been a major factor in myth-making about him.

None of this explains adequately how Nietzsche could come to be portrayed as the Man of Sorrows, or indeed in many other guises. For all his ambiguities and his careful lack of definition of an ideal, one would have thought there were limits to the extent of possible misrepresentations. All I can lamely say here is that evidently there appear to be no limits. If someone develops a reputation as vast as his rapidly became, once he was no longer in a position to do anything about it, it seems that he will be unscrupulously used to give credentials to any movement that needs an icon. Here, as in some other respects, he does with awful irony come to resemble his antipode, the 'Crucified One'. Almost the last words he wrote were, 'I have a duty against which my habits, even more the pride of my instincts, revolt at bottom: *Listen to me! For I am thus and thus. Do not, above all, confound me with what I am not!*' (*EH*, preface, 1). In the century since he wrote that, few of his readers, fewer still of those who have heard about him, have done anything else.

Chapter 2
Tragedy: Birth, Death, Rebirth

Nietzsche was a precocious student, but though he wrote copiously from an early age, his first book, *The Birth of Tragedy*, or to give the first edition its full title, *The Birth of Tragedy from the Spirit of Music*, only appeared when he was 27. Its hostile reception in the academic world, where he had received such early advancement as to be appointed Professor of Classical Philology at Basle at the age of 24, should not have surprised him; but apparently it did. It meets no conceivable standards of rigour, let alone those that obtained in the study of the ancient Greeks. A broadside soon appeared over the name of an old enemy from his schooldays, Ulrich von Wilamowitz-Moellendorf, who charged him with ignorance, distortion of the facts, and grotesque parallels between Greek culture and the modern world. Erwin Rohde, a staunch friend, replied in terms at least as pugnacious, and the kind of battle familiar in academic circles directed to those who offend against their canons ensued. Nietzsche had gained notoriety, but it was brief, and was the only kind of fame with which he was ever to be acquainted.

Readers ever since have been divided into those who find its rhapsodic style, and the content which necessitates it, intoxicating, and those who respond with bored contempt. Both are readily understandable. It is a whirlwind of a book, swept along by the intensity of its strange set of enthusiasms and its desire to cope with as many topics as possible in a short space, but masquerading as a historical account of why Greek tragedy lasted for so short a time, and arguing that it had recently been reborn in the mature works of Richard Wagner. Nietzsche had been a fanatical admirer of some of Wagner's dramas since he encountered the score of *Tristan und Isolde*, which he and some friends had played on the piano and quasi-sung when he was sixteen (*EH* 11. 6; but see also Love, 1963). And he had met the composer and his then mistress Cosima, daughter of Liszt, in 1868, becoming their close friend in 1869, and visiting them often during the years that they lived in Tribschen on Lake Lucerne. There is no doubt that the whole subject-matter of *BT* had been discussed frequently during those visits, and that Wagner contributed substantially to the development of some of its central theses (Silk and Stem, 1981: ch. 3). But when he and Cosima received their copy of the book they were nevertheless bowled over by it. However much influence Wagner, who adored pseudo-historical speculation, may have had, there was enough that was new to him in the book for him to find it a revelation.

Generally sympathetic readers of the book have often regretted that its last ten sections are largely devoted to a consideration of Wagner's art as the rebirth of Greek tragedy. Not only does the claim seem to them in itself absurd, but also they feel it detracts and distracts from the unity, such as it is, of the first two-thirds of *BT*. That is almost wholly to miss the point of the book's endeavour, and of what Nietzsche spent his life trying to do. For what makes *BT* the indispensable start to Nietzsche's writing career, for those who want to understand the underlying unity of his concerns, is the manner in which he begins with a set of issues which seem to be remote from the present time, but gradually reveals that his underlying concern is with culture, its perennial conditions, and the enemies of their fulfilment.

BT begins at a spanking pace, and the momentum never lets up. It is a good idea to read it for the first time as fast as one can, ignoring obscurities and apparent diversions from the central argument (that

8

term being used in a generously broad sense). Such an initial reading certainly involves taking a lot on trust, but to subject it to critical scrutiny the first time through is a recipe for irritation and ennui. It is important to get the sense of flux which the book possesses and which is to some extent also its subject-matter. After the 'Preface to Richard Wagner' which mentions both 'the serious German problem we are dealing with' and the conviction that 'art is the supreme task and the truly metaphysical activity of this life,' Nietzsche begins the book proper with the claim 'We shall have gained much for the science of aesthetics when we have succeeded in perceiving directly, and not only through logical reasoning, that art derives its continuous development from the duality of the *Apolline and Dionysiac*.' So within the space of a very few lines Nietzsche has shown that he is going to be advancing on three fronts. The first mentioned is that of the contemporary crisis in German culture, the second an audacious claim about the nature of metaphysics, and the third a concern with 'the science of aethetics'. (For 'science' Nietzsche uses the word 'Wissenschaft', which covers any systematic investigation, and not what is meant by 'science' in English – this should be remembered throughout his work, or indeed any discussion in German.)

He rapidly moves on to dealing with the 'opposition' between the Apolline and the Dionysiac, but that should not be taken to mean that they are enemies. As his exposition unfolds, it immediately becomes clear that 'These two very different tendencies walk side by side, usually in violent opposition to one another, inciting one another to ever more powerful births,' until they seem 'at last to beget the work of art that is as Dionysiac as it is Apolline – Attic tragedy.' This kind of opposition which yet contrives to be immensely more fruitful than anything that could be produced by either of the opponents going it alone is characteristic of nineteenth-century German philosophy, its leading exponent being Hegel, a philosopher to whom Nietzsche was in general strongly antagonistic throughout his life, no doubt in part because of his attachment to Schopenhauer, whose loathing of Hegel was notorious. But in the elaboration of the opposition and its overcoming Nietzsche does not need any of the dialectical apparatus that Hegel encumbers himself with. For he can work out his scheme by means of images and examples, and that is what he does, though the examples are often used tendentiously.

The idea is that the Apolline is the art of appearance, indeed *is* appearance. Nietzsche invokes dreams to make his point, that at its most representative Apolline art has extraordinary clarity, giving hard edges to what it depicts, exemplifying the *principium individuationis* (the principle of individuation) which Schopenhauer had located as the major error that we suffer from epistemologically – we perceive and conceive of the world in terms of separate objects, including separate persons. As beings with sense organs and conceptual apparatus, we cannot avoid this fundamentally erroneous way of viewing the world; and for Schopenhauer it is responsible for many of our most painful illusions and experiences, though it is unclear that overcoming it should lead to our lives being any less frightful.

Nietzsche traded, in *BT*, on the confusions in Schopenhauer's thought – it is nowhere evident that he was any more aware of them than Schopenhauer himself – to produce his own, somewhat independent, 'artists' metaphysics', as he contemptuously refers to his procedure in the 'Attempt at a Self-Criticism', the magnificent introduction that he wrote to the third edition of the book in 1886, the year of self-reckoning. By that phrase 'artists' metaphysics' he meant partly a metaphysics tailor-made to give art an importance that he later came to regard as preposterous; and partly the use of artistic or pseudo-artistic methods to produce metaphysical views, testing them by their beauty rather than for their truth. One way of looking at *BT* is as a transcendental argument, in Kant's sense. What that comes to in general is the following pattern: x is the case – the datum. What else must be the case in order for that (x) to be possible? Nietzsche's datum is very unlike that found in any other philosopher, since it gives primacy to our aesthetic experience, normally low on the list of philosophical priorities, when it figures at all. He takes the experiences we have of Apolline art (sculpture, painting, above all the epic) and Dionysiac art (music, tragedy) as his data, and asks how the world must be in order for these experiences to be vouchsafed us. We have seen that he compares Apolline art to dreams; Dionysiac art is aligned rather, as a first indication of its nature, with intoxication, the low way in which the principle of individuation is felt to be overcome, the loss of clarity, and the merging of individualities.

Why do we need them both, once we have grasped that one is the representation of beautiful appearance, while the other enables us to experience reality so far as we can without being destroyed by it? Because we are so constructed that doses of reality must be reserved for special occasions, as the Greeks realized: for festivals (the first Bayreuth Festival was being planned while Nietzsche wrote, though it would not materialize until 1876). But there is more to it than that. There is nothing wrong with appearances, so long as we realize that that is what they are (this will always be a leading motif in Nietzsche's work). As we saw, the Greek epic is an Apolline art form, and its proudest manifestation is of course the *Iliad*, a work that delights us with its lucidity and its hard edges. The Greeks who lived it were happy to make for themselves fictions of a realm of gods enjoying themselves at their expense – 'the only satisfactory form of theodicy', Nietzsche remarks memorably (*BT* 3). And at this level the formula which occurs twice in the first edition, and is repeated approvingly in the 'Attempt at a Self-Criticism', operates: 'Only as an aesthetic phenomenon is the world justified' (the formulations vary slightly). Since for the Greeks of the Homeric age existence on its barest terms would have been intolerable, they showed a heroic artistic instinct in turning their battle-bound lives into a spectacle. That is why they needed gods; not to console themselves with the thought of a better life hereafter, which has been the usual motivation for postulating another world, but to mark the distinction between any life they could lead and the immortal lives of the gods, who just because they were immortal could be as reckless and irresponsible as Homer shockingly, to us, shows them being. 'Anyone who approaches these Olympians with a different religion in his heart, seeking elevated morals, even sanctity, ethereal spirituality, charity and mercy, will quickly be forced to turn his back on them, discouraged and disappointed' (*BT* 3).

If we can give a sense, any longer, to the concept of the heroic – something about which Nietzsche had lifelong doubts – it is surely in getting an imaginative grasp on such a vision. This is Nietzsche's first attempt to give force to a phrase that he became addicted to in his later work, 'a pessimism of strength'. He was never callow enough to be an optimist, to think that life would ever become, in a way that a non-hero could appreciate it, wonderful. We, as non-heroes, can only concern ourselves with improving 'the quality of life' (one wishes Nietzsche were around to give what would be the only adequate comment on that appalling phrase). If we feel that it cannot be improved, we become pessimists, but sentimental, or as Nietzsche came to call it 'Romantic' ones, lamenting the miseries of life, and perhaps putting our laments into suitably emollient poetic form.

Nietzsche's celebration of Homer and the heroes to whom he gave his version of immortality by writing the *Iliad* is enough to show that there is nothing intrinsically wrong with Apolline art. But it connives in an illusion, and so is inherently unstable, liable to lapse into something less worthy. As the Greeks became more aware of their relationship to the gods, the age of the epic, which refuses to probe where trouble is likely to be the outcome, gave rise to the age of the tragic. There are many ways in which Nietzsche expresses this momentous transition, most of them influenced by his passionate but short-lived discipleship of Schopenhauer. At the end of section 1 of *BT* he writes: 'Man is no longer an artist [as he had been in creating the gods], he has become a work of art: the artistic power of the whole of nature reveals itself to the supreme gratification of the primal Oneness amidst the paroxysms of intoxication.' At this still early point in *BT* we have the feeling, thrilled or exasperated according to our temperament, that Nietzsche is making it all up as he goes along. He has had a large number of profound and moving artistic experiences, not very many of other kinds, and he is trying to make sense of them in the only way a great critic, at least since the collapse of the Classical tradition in criticism, can do: by composing a work which seems, in its essential movement, to duplicate the strength and richness of those experiences.

In such a mode of procedure, words and phrases come first, then you think what you mean by them. It is a procedure which Nietzsche would use all his writing life, but would soon realize was not fitted to the mode of expression typical of a monograph with the appurtenances of an academic treatise. The passage that I quoted immediately above is a good example of that. Having characterized the Homeric Greeks as artists, thanks to their creative capacities with respect to inventing capricious deities (capacities that they had to have to endure life) he moves on to the idea that they become works of art themselves, but the movement is in the first place on the level of playing with words for a serious purpose. Then he has to justify it, having first explained what it means. The Schopenhauerian notion (which provided the framework in which his thinking could be done) that underlying all individual appearances is a single, fundamentally unchanging Oneness comes to his rescue, and he celebrates the tragedy-producing Greeks for making men into works of art, or in his alternative formulation, 'artists of life'. They realize that to confront reality instead of loving beautiful appearances they must cope with the fact that life is *au fond* eternally destructive of the individual, and allow themselves to abandon their separateness, delighting in the Dionysiac art which was their strong-hold against the Dionysiac festivals of the barbarians, at the centre of which 'was an extravagant want of sexual discipline, whose waves engulfed all the venerable rules of family life. The most savage beasts of nature were here unleashed, even that repellent mixture of love and cruelty that I have always held to be a "witches' brew" ' (*BT* 2).

Art, that is, always, even at its most Dionysiac, possesses form, and thus up to a point falsifies its subject-matter, which is a formless swirl of pain-cum-pleasure, with pain predominating. But it needs to perform this falsification, for otherwise we would find it unendurable. Thus much later in the book when he is discussing Wagner's *Tristan und Isolde*, Nietzsche claims that it has to be a drama, because in dramas there are characters, i.e. individuals, which means that Apollo is playing his part. In Act III of the drama, Tristan the character interposes between us and Wagner's music; Tristan mediates the experience which causes him to die, and we survive, having come as close as possible to direct contact with the primal reality. So tragic heroes are sacrificial victims, and we achieve 'redemption', a favourite term of Wagner's as well as of Christians, which Nietzsche was shortly to regret having used, though in other contexts it went on serving his purpose.

I have vaulted over the intervening chapters of *BT* in order to show how Nietzsche tries to establish a continuity between Greek tragedy and Wagnerian music drama. The latter is bound, he thinks, to mean more to us than the former can because the music to which the Greek tragedies were performed has been lost, so we can only infer their effects from accounts of how their audiences responded to them: they were put into a state of *Rausch* (intoxication) which is only now once more available to us. This state is impossible except to a community of spectators, whose sense of loss of identity is an upmarket version of that felt by a contemporary football crowd. But we have to concentrate on the way that *Rausch is* produced, otherwise there will be no qualitative distinction between a football crowd and the audience at a tragedy. Before long Nietzsche came to feel, for complex reasons, that there was no significant distinction between an audience of Wagnerians and his equivalent of a band of lager louts. But that thought lay in the painful future. For the present he was intent on the regeneration of the spirit of community thanks to its members being united in a common ecstasy. That is 'the seriously German problem

14

that we are dealing with', Nietzsche at this stage taking it that the Germans were the possessors of a sensitivity to ultimate truths and values which other nations are denied, thanks in large part to the richness of the Germans' musical inheritance.

In between his opening statements about the duality of Apollo and Dionysus and the extraordinarily involved dialectic in which they fertilize one another in the closing sections of the book we get Nietzsche's highly, not to say grotesquely, schematized version of the peaks (Aeschylus and Sophocles) and decline (Euripides) of Greek tragedy. His central thesis is that in the peaks the chorus predominates, so that the audience sees on stage its own reflection, raised to overpowering heights of suffering and transfiguration. But when Euripides, whose plays unfortunately survive in far greater numbers than those of his superior predecessors, arrives on the scene he manifests an interest in individuals, in psychology, and worst of all in the beneficial effects of rationality, or as Nietzsche tends to call it, 'dialectic'. Nietzsche has no doubts that the corrupting influence on him was Socrates, fully deserving his hemlock not for his power over the youth of Athens, but over what might have been its continuing tragic greatness. 'Euripides became the poet of aesthetic Socratism' (*BT* 12).

The characteristic that makes Socrates so radically anti-tragic a figure is his belief in the omnipotence of reason – though one might point out that in the dialogues of Plato which scholars regard as most likely to be accounts of Socrates' own views, not much progress is made, except of a negative kind. But Nietzsche's portrayal of him survives this point:

> In this quite abnormal character, instinctive wisdom appears only to *hinder* conscious knowledge at certain points. While in all productive people instinct is the power of creativity and affirmation, and consciousness assumes a critical and dissuasive role, in Socrates instinct

15

becomes the critic, consciousness the creator – a monstrosity *per defectum*!

(BT 13)

The image of Socrates was never to let Nietzsche free; as with all the leading characters in his pantheon and anti-pantheon, his relationship with him remains one of tortured ambivalence. For Nietzsche did not think that the relationship between instinct and consciousness was as simple as he here pretends to. What he was sure of was

> the optimistic element in dialectic, which rejoices at each conclusion and can breathe only in cool clarity and consciousness: that optimistic element which, once it had invaded tragedy, gradually overgrew its Dionysiac regions and forced itself into self-destruction – its death-leap into bourgeois theatre. We need only consider the Socratic maxims: 'Virtue is knowledge, all sins arise from ignorance, the virtuous man is the happy man.' In these three basic optimistic formulae lies the death of tragedy.

(BT 14)

It is a brilliant indictment, even if it has very little to do with Euripides. For it can be no accident that the great tradition of rationalism in Western philosophy has gone with an amazing uniformity of optimism, nor that we have to wait until Schopenhauer to encounter a philosopher who is a pessimist, and going with that an anti-rationalist, believing in the primacy of an irrational Will. The Western tradition has been inimical to tragedy, thanks to the co-operation of Platonism and Christianity, and its great tragedies, above all those of Shakespeare and Racine, are either removed from a theological context or in uneasy relationship to it. Not that Nietzsche is able to countenance Shakespeare as a fully-fledged tragedian, because of the absence of music. This puts him in an awkward position, which he deals with by almost total evasion. The one briefly sustained passage on Shakespeare in *BT* is brilliantly perceptive on Hamlet, as being a man who, having

Nietzsche

looked into the Dionysiac abyss, realizes the futility of all action – he is not a delayer but a despairer (*BT* 7). But how that can have the full tragic effect, if it does, is not something that he explores.

More damagingly still, Nietzsche does nothing to explain why there are so few musical tragedies; he seems to take it for granted that Wagner wrote them, though it seems clear to me that he did not. Indeed, one composer after another has used the sovereign powers of music to show that, however bad things may be on stage, they can be saved. What really impressed Nietzsche was the degree of ecstasy which music, unlike any other art, can induce. And since he accorded a traditionally high status to tragedy, as the art form which shows how we can survive even the apparently unendurable, he effected an amalgam of the two.

It is here that his allegiance to Schopenhauer is most damaging. For Schopenhauer too believed that music gives us direct access to the movements of the Will, since it is unmediated by concepts. But on his general account of the nature of the Will, eternally striving and necessarily never achieving, it is hard to see how or why we should take any pleasure in an art which puts us in immediate contact with it. One would have thought that the greater distance there is between us and reality, the less tormented we would be.

Nietzsche modifies Schopenhauer somewhat by claiming that the Primal One is a mixture of pain and pleasure, but as stated above pain predominates. What Nietzsche is doing is attempting to answer the traditional question: Why do we enjoy tragedy? He rightly dissociates himself from the traditional answers, viewing them as shallow and complacent. But in his effort to erect tragedy into an agent which transfigures the seemingly untransfigurable, he overshoots the mark, appearing himself to fall into the trap of equating the true and the beautiful, something which he later excoriated in satisfyingly vigorous terms. We want to ask him the question at this point that he was not to ask until more than a decade later: Why truth rather than untruth? What is it in us that urges us always to seek the truth?

It is not as if he has no answers to these questions in *BT*, but they remain obscure. And we shall not find him getting fully to the bottom of these issues until his last phase. What is noteworthy, though, is that he is already embarking on the central quest of his life: How can existence be made bearable, once we grasp what it is really like? The way he approaches it here is by quoting early on a story about Silenus, friend of Dionysus, who said 'Miserable, ephemeral race, children of hazard and hardship, why do you force me to say what it would be much more fruitful for you not to hear? The best of all things is something entirely outside your grasp: not to be born, not to be, to be nothing. But the second-best for you is to die soon' (*BT* 3). But though Silenus is 'wise', ultimately tragic wisdom (Nietzsche is constantly opposing *Wissenschaft* (knowledge, science) and *Weisheit* (wisdom), manages to trump even him. It does so, according to some pretty esoteric manoeuvres executed late in the book, by an elaborate interplay between the Apolline and the Dionysiac. Then comes his most suggestive remark: 'The pleasure produced by the tragic myth has the same origin as the pleasurable perception of dissonance in music. The Dionysiac, with its primal pleasure experienced even in pain, is the common womb of music and the tragic myth' (*BT* 24).

One might feel that this is what Schoenberg later called 'the emancipation of the dissonance' with a vengeance. For though we find music without dissonances to be resolved insipid, the world seems to present us rather with incessant dissonance, with odd moments of respite. But it is no good pressing the point at this stage. Nietzsche is indeed providing us with an artist's metaphysic, in which the recalcitrance of the material to be organized is a stimulus to ever-greater feats of creation – but a creation that is also an imitation, so that we can say both that we are presented with reality, but that through being given form it is transformed.

At the beginning of the *Duino Elegies*, Rilke writes: 'For Beauty is nothing / but the beginning of terror, which we are still just able to endure, / and we are so awed by it because it serenely disdains to annihilate us' (trans. by Stephen Mitchell, slightly modified). That, one could fairly say, is the basic thought of *BT*. It is at the least disturbing, and may even be felt to be disgusting (Young, 1992: 54–5). It decisively obliterates the long-held distinction between the Sublime and the Beautiful, making the former into an all-important element in the latter. But that may be the least striking of its innovations. More significantly, it announces the determination which Nietzsche maintained throughout his career, and manifested heroically in his life, not to give pain an automatically negative role in life, something which he perhaps felt more oppressed by in the contemporary scene than anything else. At the same time, he was possessed by a vision of the world as a place of such horror that any attempt to give meaning to it in moral terms is simply impossible. That is why in the 'Attempt at a Self-Criticism', having criticized the book more harshly than anyone else had done, saying that he found it 'impossible', he still finds that 'it already betrays a spirit which will defy all risks to oppose the *moral* interpretation and significance of existence' (*BT*, 'Attempt at a Self-Criticism', 5). And a few lines further on he specifies 'Christianity as the most extravagant elaboration of the moral theme that humanity has ever heard.' Though there is hindsight operating here, it is true that he was always sensitive enough to suffering (other people's – he was an incredible stoic about his own) to find an 'explanation' of it in terms of the good it does us, its being a retribution for our wrongdoings, and the rest of the clap-trap that rings down through the millennia intolerable.

BT may well be most of the awful things Nietzsche and others have accused it of, but it has proved a fecund source of inspiration for Classical scholars and anthropologists. It is also, thanks to its highlighting of the Apolline – Dionysiac duality, a book that has had a powerful influence on the vulgar imagination. It gains, too, from rereading; once one has the general movement clear, there are many particular insights that are not to be found elsewhere in Nietzsche. But it will never repay a certain kind of close reading, that which is in vogue today and looks for aporias, fissures, self-subversions, and the rest of the deconstructionist's tool-kit. Only books which apparently achieve a consistency of thought which *BT* undeniably lacks will do that. Its consistency is to be found only in the enthusiasm with which Nietzsche is determined to weld together in a process of feeling his most cherished concerns, and his idols as manifesting them. It is, in other words, a young man's book, less candid than his later ones about its closeness to its author. And, perhaps most strikingly, it is the most optimistic expression of a pessimistic world-view that has ever been penned.

Chapter 3
Disillusionment and Withdrawal

The years which culminated in the writing of *BT* were the happiest in
Nietzsche's life, indeed the last that were not dogged by ill health,
loneliness, and rejection. When the Wagners left Tribschen and moved
to Bayreuth in 1872 Nietzsche's most consistently warm and fruitful
relationship(s) were at an end. Without Wagner's presence, Nietzsche
began to have doubts about the quality and purpose of his music
dramas, on which he meditated to the end of his life. But he was still
officially a Wagnerian, recruited to produce more propaganda for a
cause that badly needed it. Anxious about the state of German culture,
which he soon began to feel he had vastly overrated in *BT*, he
embarked on a series of tracts for the times, therefore called *Untimely
Meditations*. Thirteen were projected, but only four were written.
Probably that is two too many. Upwards of fifty pages in length, as
long essays, they show Nietzsche failing to discover a form that is
suited to his gifts. Trying to expound and develop an argument in a
manner less ecstatic than *BT*, he resorts for the only time in his life to
diffuseness and padding.

But there is a more basic problem with *UM* than those. While he directs
himself to assessing the health of contemporary culture, with an attack
on the aged David Strauss, author of *The Life of Jesus*, but more
perniciously for Nietzsche, of *The Old Faith and the New*; to the practice
of historiography; and then to celebrations of the genius of

Schopenhauer and Wagner, he had not, with the signal exception of the Second Meditation, 'On the uses and disadvantages of history for life', found subjects which coincided sufficiently closely with his concerns. The book by Strauss that he selects for critique in the First Meditation is so undemanding a pewside read, so unresisting an object for intelligent scorn, that one wonders why Nietzsche is bothering, and evidently so does he. Even so, it is worth reading through; it deals with very much the same topics as Matthew Arnold's *Culture and Anarchy*, and the most profitable way of reading it is side by side with that shallow and influential pamphlet, whose terminology it shares to a surprising degree. And it does contain one of Nietzsche's most inspired coinages, 'philistine of culture', the man who knows about what he should, and makes sure that it has no effect on him.

The Second Meditation is a great work, a real meditation on the extent to which we can cope with the burden of knowledge, specifically historical knowledge, and still manage to be our own men. And it ends with a rousing appeal to us to embrace the Greek concept of culture as opposed to the Roman, the former being that 'of culture as new and improved Nature [*physis*], without inner and outer, without dissimulation and convention, culture as a unanimity of life, thought, appearance and will' (*UM* 2. 10). Excellent, but there is a speech-day quality about these sentiments that nothing in the body of the essay does much to fill out.

The Third Meditation, 'Schopenhauer as Educator', is bewildering mainly because it is so little concerned with Schopenhauer. Nietzsche's discipleship of the compromised pessimist was waning, and what he chiefly has to praise about him is his scorn of university philosophers, but Schopenhauer had done it far better himself in Parerga and Paralipomena. The last Meditation, 'Richard Wagner in Bayreuth', makes painful reading. Even if we had no idea that Nietzsche was, while he wrote it, simultaneously entering in his notebooks grave questions about Wagner, we would feel something was wrong. It is the only occasion on which Nietzsche sounds insincere, trying to recapture a state of mind which had been wonderful while it lasted, but was moving with alarming speed into the past. The only explanation for Wagner's enthusiasm for it – 'Friend, how did you get to know me so well?' – is that he was too busy to read it. It makes, in its way, a fitting prelude to the next crucial event (one of the few) in Nietzsche's life: his attendance at the first Bayreuth Festival in 1876, and the break with Wagner.

Most of Nietzsche's commentators greet with relief his becoming an anti-Wagnerian, possibly because they think it exempts them from knowing anything much about Wagner. Of course it does nothing of the kind, since Wagner is the person who continues to feature more often in Nietzsche's writings than anyone else, including Socrates, Christ, or Goethe. But at a serious level they may feel that Nietzsche was not being true to himself when he was a Wagnerian, and became true to himself by causing the extremely painful rift, of which Wagner was not even aware for a long time. To decide what were, in order of importance, the factors which led to it is impossible. No doubt Nietzsche's naïve expectations of what the Bayreuth Festival would be like were shatteringly disappointed; so were Wagner's, but he knew what the practicalities of the situation were. The books had to be balanced, though they disastrously were not; but the attempt meant that the well-heeled had to be wooed, that what was intended to be a festival in which the community celebrated their shared values at minimal cost turned into something in which the fashionable world of philistines of culture was most in evidence, along with crowned heads and other irrelevances.

Nietzsche, horrified by the company, fled into the nearby countryside to recover from his eclipsing headaches. There, and later, he took stock of his relationship with Wagner the man and the artist. He was certainly now in a mood where he did not want to be anyone's disciple, and that must have been a key factor. He may have been in love with

Cosima; the evidence is inconclusive but makes the idea reasonable. The least convincing explanation is the one on which Nietzsche put most public weight – that Wagner had become a Christian. Receiving the poem of *Parsifal* was allegedly the last straw. But he had been present in 1869 when Wagner read out the prose sketch, and had heard Wagner talking about the subject, so it cannot have been the bombshell that he claimed it was. Not to be discounted are Nietzsche's own ambitions as a composer, the most embarrassing of his failures. A man who could play his own amateur piano pieces to Wagner, and who could continue to write, until much later, choral pieces that sound like Congregational Church hymns with a few wrong notes but are called 'Hymn to Life' or 'Hymn to Friendship' was evidently not able to judge his own gifts in this respect.

And it is not only as a composer that Nietzsche was frustrated. He was in a comprehensive way, a creative artist *manqué*. That accounts in large measure for the cavalier way in which he treats the great artists, even the ones he most admires, throughout his work. He is the most distinguished member of that class of writers, who at their best are incomparably insightful, at their worst arrogant and merely distorting; who, unable to produce art themselves, ransack other people's in order to purvey their own vision. Perhaps all the great critics (a very small class in any case) are like that. One certainly does not go to them for accurate accounts of the works with which they deal – that can be left to merely very good critics. But seeing the great artists, whose images in any case tend to become marmoreal as they are routinely categorized as 'classics', in the light of a fervent imagination providing a strange and highly 'interested' slant on them, is exhilarating. It probably accounts better than anything else for the continuing impact of such works as *BT*.

Perhaps the most helpful way to look at the break is that in Wagner Nietzsche had, for the only time in his life, met one of his symbols in the flesh. It is clear from *BT* onwards that almost all proper names in his texts stand not for individuals, but for movements, tendencies, ways of living. This characteristic of Nietzsche's is frequently inspired, occasionally perverse and misleading. The confusion in Wagner's case is that for him Wagner did, in the first place, mean a person with whom he had a 'star friendship' (*GS*), and he was not able to separate, in his writings, what Wagner was from what he came to stand for, so that the degree of ambivalence he shows towards him exceeds that of his other hero-villains. If he had never met Wagner he would still almost inevitably have given him an important role in his works, because Wagner does sum up for him, in the most convenient way, traits in late nineteenth-century culture to which he was mostly bitterly opposed, though not as single-mindedly as he would have liked to be. But the loss of Wagner as friend and mentor, though it was necessary, cost Nietzsche more than he was ever able to come to terms with.

Nietzsche dealt with his problems in the only way that was ever available to him: he wrote prodigiously, producing a new book that in nearly all respects shows his fast-growing powers, and in the mode that from now on most of what he composed would be in. *Human, All Too Human*, subtitled 'A book for free spirits', is in nine books, with very general titles, and 638 numbered sections, many with their own titles (he was later to publish two very substantial sequels, so that the whole volume is by far the largest of his books). As with all books written in this mode, it makes exhausting reading. Even though the sections are grouped together according to subject-matter, Nietzsche allows himself plenty of latitude, so one is bombarded with particular points which are displaced by others at such a rate that the result is, to one's dismay, unmemorable. The only way is to mark the sections that make a special impact, and return to them later. It is a crucial element in Nietzsche's strategy of writing, though a risky one. Its deployment so lavishly and so suddenly in his writing is the expression of his revulsion from the pseudo-narrative of *BT*, a book easy to remember despite its turgidity, simply because it does have a connecting thread.

But for all its perennial freshness, there is something about *HAH* which leads one to feel that Nietzsche is not working at the level which is naturally his. The dedication to Voltaire is a warning. For although Voltaire's breezy superficiality was what Nietzsche may have felt he wanted after the sustained effort to plumb the depths of Romantic pessimism, it is hard to think of two temperaments more essentially opposed. *Candide*, Voltaire's critique of optimism, is itself an ineliminably upbeat book. What appealed to Nietzsche in him, as in the French aphorists of the seventeenth century, was the hardness of their style, an Apolline quality which suggests that experience can be tied up in neat, eye-catching little parcels. All good aphoristic writing is tiring to read, because one has to do so much of the writer's work for him. He supplies a sentence, the reader turns it into a paragraph. Nietzsche wrote that he wanted to say in a page what anyone else would take a book to express – and what they even then would not have succeeded in expressing. But the kind of aphorisms and quasi-aphorisms that he aspired to write were ones that would have the effect of transforming the reader's consciousness: in other words, they would have the opposite effect from those of, say, La Rochefoucauld. Nietzsche, at his most characteristic and best, is always producing the reverse of an encapsulation of experience: his subversions, teasings, and insults are directed towards making us feel ashamed not only of how we are, but also of our complacency in thinking that we possess the best set of categories for the realization of what we might be. They are not weary, nor do they induce weariness, because they lead us to an enhanced sense of the possibilities of escape from the routine of being ourselves. It has been characteristic of the French tradition of moralists that they are observers, reporting elegantly on the perennial human condition. They provide *frissons* of shame in the reader, but no expectation that he might ever be different.

So Nietzsche's lengthy flirtation with them was more a matter of how they said things than of what they said. But that suggests something odd: for he is a stickler for the indissolubility of form and content, from

26

the beginning to the end. How else could he have placed such a weight on genre in *BT*, where the fact that a work is a drama rather than an epic poem makes the whole difference to its impact? It can only be explained by his extreme turning-away from Romanticism: everything now had to be seen in the clear light of day, at the same time that it should be infinitely suggestive. In *HAH* he is more preoccupied with the former than the latter, and the result is that one feels, certainly in the light of his later work, that he is constraining himself, surveying the scene – human nature in its manifestations as social life, passion, the psychology of artists, solitude – without the will to transform which is his defining characteristic. So, to take at random one of his *aperçus*:

> *Thirst for profound pain.* – When it has passed, passion leaves behind an obscure longing for itself and even in departing casts a seductive glance. To be scourged by it must have afforded us a kind of joy. The milder sensations, on the other hand, appear insipid; it seems we always prefer the more vehement displeasure to a feeble pleasure.
>
> (*HAH* I. 606)

That is quite deep, and produces a sense, rather than a shock, of recognition. Elsewhere the accuracy can be painful: '*Compelling oneself to pay attention.* – As soon as we notice that anyone has to *compel* himself to pay attention when associating and talking with us, we have a valid proof that he does not love us or loves us no longer' (*HAH* II. 247).

Writing *HAH*, a book which Wagner said, on receiving his signed copy of it, Nietzsche would one day thank him for not reading, revealed to Nietzsche some aspects of himself he must have been pleased to discover. First, that he belonged to that rare breed on whom nothing is wasted. His range of experience was, in many respects, extraordinarily narrow, but it was adequate for him to view his culture and his acquaintances and produce unnervingly comprehensive accounts of them. In *Ecce Homo*, his bizarre autobiography in which the mood alternates vertiginously between the apocalyptic and the parodistic, he congratulates himself on the possession of a remarkably fine nose, an organ that philosophers have tended to give short shrift to. The first devastating manifestation of its acuteness is in *HAH*. Secondly, it showed him that even under conditions as miserable and deprived as he was in he could work at a level of brilliance which was self-generating. As in *BT*, one feels that it is the momentum of the writing that generates much of what is most impressive in it. Thirdly, and most significant, he was able to dwell on subjects which had occasioned fearful pain and not exhibit the least degree of rancour; *HAH* is a work in which he demonstrates, what he had not yet advocated, that it is possible to turn the most harrowing things that happen to good purposes, and exhibit high spirits without advertising to us that that is what he is doing, a trying tendency in some of his later works.

His next book, *Daybreak*, subtitled 'Thoughts on the Prejudices of Morality', continues the mode of *HAH*, but marks a crucial departure in content, and is much more of a piece with his later works. In between 1878, when *HAH* was published, to universal indifference, and 1880, when he wrote *D*, his pattern of life changed drastically, and the way in which he was to live for the next decade began. Most of his friends were bewildered by his change of direction, and he was alienated from all but the most loyal. In 1879, several years too late, he resigned his professorship at Basle, students having lost all interest in his teaching. In that year, too, he had 118 days of severe migraine, rendering him incapable of work. His health had been undermined by the combined attacks of dysentery and diphtheria which he had sustained in 1870, when serving as a medical orderly in the Franco-Prussian War; and it seems most likely that he contracted syphilis from a prostitute sometime in the late 1870s when he was in Italy, which led to his eventual insanity and paralysis. From then on he led a nomadic existence, looking for places which would alleviate his sickness, and permit him the maximum amount of solitude for writing. His preferred places were the towns of northern Italy in the winter, and the Swiss

Alps in the summer, though it was not until 1882 that that became his annual routine.

Nietzsche proffers some advice on how to read *D*, though it comes late in the book; 'A book such as this is not for reading straight through or reading aloud but for dipping into, especially when out walking or on a journey; you must be able to stick your head into it and out of it again and again and discover nothing familiar around you' (*D* 454). Which is all very well, but if taken seriously might result in one's never reading it all through. So once more it is a good idea to canter through it, and then to take Nietzsche's advice, if at all. But it is not really good advice, and is probably even meant sarcastically. For this, one of Nietzsche's least studied books, is where he gets back on to the high road of his life's endeavour. It might even seem that it is where he properly begins it, but that is to overlook the extent to which *BT* set the agenda.

Chapter 4
Morality and its Discontents

Nietzsche's fundamental concern throughout his life was to plot the relationship between suffering and culture, or cultures. He categorizes and grades cultures by the way in which they have coped with the omnipresence of suffering, and assesses moralities by the same criterion. That is why he was interested in tragedy, but lost interest when he came to feel that it was not a contemporary possibility. It is why he was always passionately preoccupied with the heroic, in life rather than art, and needing eventually to be rebaptized as the *Übermensch* (I shall leave this word untranslated, since I find 'superman' absurd, and 'overman' unnatural). It is the basis of his attack on transcendent metaphysics, and on all religions that postulate an afterlife. And, of course, it was of primary 'existential' concern to him, because his life was suffering.

Correlative with this preoccupation with how one regards suffering is Nietzsche's interest in greatness rather than goodness. For there is no greatness without a readiness and capacity to withstand, absorb, and use to best purpose an immense quantity of pain. Greatness, one might say to anticipate, involves putting pain to work; goodness involves attempting to eliminate it. All Nietzsche's later works will be devoted to exploring this profound difference. In *D* he presents his first, by no means tentative, analyses of the mechanisms of morality, and of the kind of authority it invokes.

To avoid misunderstanding, it will be useful to quote at length a passage from *D*, which undercuts many of the criticisms that are often made of Nietzsche:

> *There are two kinds of deniers of morality*. – 'To deny morality' – this can mean, *first*: to deny that the moral motives which men claim have inspired their actions really have done so – it is thus the assertion that morality consists of words and is among the coarser or more subtle deceptions (especially self-deceptions) which men practise, and is perhaps so especially in precisely the case of those most famed for virtue. *Then* it can mean: to deny that moral judgements are based on truths. Here it is admitted that they really are motives of action, but that in this way it is *errors* which, as the basis of all moral judgment, impel men to their moral actions. This is my point of view: though I should be the last to deny that in very many cases there is some ground for suspicion that the other point of view – that is to say, the point of view of La Rochefoucauld and others who think like him – may also be justified and in any event of great general application. Thus I deny morality as I deny alchemy, that is, I deny their premises: but I do not deny that there have been alchemists who believed in these premises and acted in accordance with them – I also deny immorality: not that countless people feel themselves to be immoral, but that there is any true reason so to feel. It goes without saying that I do not deny – unless I am a fool – that many actions called immoral ought to be avoided and resisted, or that many called moral ought to be done and encouraged – but I think that the one should be encouraged and the other avoided *for other reasons than hitherto*. We have to *learn to think differently* – in order at last, perhaps very late on, to attain even more: *to feel differently*.

(*D* 103)

It is a pity that what Nietzsche tells us 'goes without saying' is something that he thereby rarely bothered to reiterate. For it is a vulgarly and widely held view that he did deny that 'many actions called immoral ought to be avoided and resisted,' etc. Note, though, that in this very careful piece of writing – it is typical of *D*, and makes it all the more surprising that it is so rarely referred to – he does say 'many' actions, but fails to specify which. That is partly, I think, because his views were undergoing radical development at this time, and he may not have wished to commit himself in certain cases. But he is, at this stage, unsure too about how far withdrawing the 'premises' of morality was going to alter the conclusions. Among the premises that he immediately goes on to attack are those which define the goal of morality in terms of 'the preservation and advancement of mankind,' about which he asks

> Can one deduce from it with certainty whether what is to be kept in view is the longest possible existence of mankind? Or the greatest possible deanimalisation of mankind? How different the means, that is to say the practical morality, would have to be in the two cases! . . . Or suppose one conceived the attainment of mankind's 'highest happiness' as being the *to what* and *of what* of morality: would one mean the highest degree of happiness that individual men could possibly attain to? Or a – necessarily incalculable – average happiness which could finally be attained by all? And why should the way to that have to be morality?

(*D* 106)

He keeps going at this furious pace, leaving the hapless commentator wondering whether to expound in detail, a valuable enterprise which would result in a very large book, but no larger than the ones awarded many times over to such worthless works as Kant's *Critique of Practical Reason*, surely the most shattering disappointment in the history of philosophy, coming after the *Critique of Pure Reason*, one of its greatest glories. Anyway, that is impossible here. The main thrust of *D*, which also has, as always, reflections on a vast range of subjects, among which contemporary music looms large, is to demonstrate the mess that morality is in. As he puts it succinctly: ' "*Utilitarian*". – Moral

sensibilities are nowadays at such cross-purposes that to one man a
morality is proved by its utility, while to another its utility refutes it'
(*D* 230).

What is notable about *D is* the restraint and the modesty of its
claims. There is no hint that Zarathustra will soon come down from
his mountain, smashing all our moral tablets. Most of the points
that it makes seem to me ungainsayable, but clearly that is not
how they strike everyone. Thus we still find plenty of people,
philosophers among them, who claim, for instance, that morality
is a self-supporting system, resting on nothing outside itself; that
morality is founded in reason, and that the basis of morality is
demonstrable; that, as Nietzsche says, a morality is proved by its
utility, or that it is refuted by it. To argue at length about these
issues is important, but would be beside the point in considering
Nietzsche's development. For all the debates that are current, at
least in the anglophone world, about morality assume a great deal
that Nietzsche denies. None of them, so far as I am aware, is
prepared to see how the various somewhat differing codes of
morality that we encounter arise from conflicting views about
the nature of the world. It is astonishing, for example, to hear
philosophers talking about their 'intuitions' as something to be
trusted and left unscrutinized, unless they come into conflict
with one another. 'My intuitions are that . . .' is a common way to
begin a philosophical discussion, as if one represented the eternal
voice of mankind.

It is on this basis, too, if not of one's own intuitions, then of those that
'we' share, that many of Nietzsche's moral positions are routinely
dismissed, as being 'elitist', 'anti-democratic', and so forth. This is such
a vital issue, and one which must be coped with by any Nietzschean
commentator, that I shall quote, also at length, from Henry Staten,
who has written what I regard as all told the most illuminating book on
Nietzsche:

Our moral beliefs did not fall from heaven and neither are they credentials we can flash like a badge to establish our moral probity. Consider all the rest of human history, including most of the planet at the present moment. What are we to say about this overwhelming spectacle of cruelty, stupidity, and suffering? What stance is there for us to adopt with respect to history, what judgment can we pass on it? Is it all a big mistake? Christianity attempted to recuperate the suffering of history by projecting a divine plan that assigns it a reason in the here and now and a recompense later, but liberalism is too humane to endorse this explanation. There is no explanation, only the brute fact. But the brute fact we are left with is even harder to stomach than the old explanation. So Left liberalism packages it in a new narrative, a moral narrative according to which all those lives ground up in the machinery of history are assigned an intelligible role as victims of oppression and injustice. There is an implicit teleology in this view; modern Left liberalism is the telos that gives form and meaning to the rest of history. Only very recently is it possible for someone like Schutte [Ofelia Schutte, who in her book *Beyond Nihilism: Nietzsche Without Masks* castigates Nietzsche for his authoritarianism] to write as she does, with so much confidence that the valuations she assumes will be received as a matter of course by an academic audience, just as much as a Christian homilist writing for an audience of the pious. And only within the protective enclosure of this community of belief can there be any satisfaction in the performance of this speech act, any sense that anything worthwhile has been accomplished by the recitation. When this moral community by means of such recitation reassures itself of its belief, it comes aglow as the repository of the meaning of history, as the locus that one may occupy in order to view history and pass judgment on it without merely despairing or covering one's eyes and ears. There may not be any plan behind history, nor any way of making up their losses to the dead, but we can draw an invisible line of rectitude through history and in this way take power over it. Against the awesome 'Thus it was' of history we set the overawing majesty of 'Thus it *ought* to have been.'

But our liberalism is something that sprang up yesterday and could be gone tomorrow. The day before yesterday the Founding Fathers kept black slaves. What little sliver of light is this we occupy that despite its contingency, the frailty of its existence, enables us to illuminate all the past and perhaps the future as well? For we want to say that even though our community of belief may cease to exist, this would not affect the validity of those beliefs. The line of rectitude would still traverse history.

(Staten, 1990: 78-9)

Staten is at pains to make clear, after this immensely impressive passage, that he is not criticizing liberalism on a relativistic basis, but only reinforcing Nietzsche's point about the contingency of our historical position, and thus of our values. This must mean that it is not enough to carry out the rituals of horror at his later views, but that they need to be seen as part of an economy of values in terms of which he, in a lonely way, and thus in a frequently and increasingly strident tone, tries to cope with life.

Even though *BT* takes up a spectator's view of tragedy, in part because it is dealing with the dramatic form rather than with human history, it emerges clearly enough that for Nietzsche the dreadfulness of existence is a perpetually present fact. 'Only as an aesthetic phenomenon is life justified' – but we must recall that Nietzsche also says, in the same book, that we ourselves are to become part of the phenomenon. There is not 'life' and then us with ringside seats. If he had thought that in 1871, he would soon be taught his mistake in the most devastating way.

And morality, meaning the variety of attitudes that we find officially espoused in our society? It ministers to our welfare, in its basic form, so that at least we feel safe when our backs are turned on other people. There is no denying that – that is what Nietzsche means by saying he does not deny that many actions called immoral ought to be avoided, etc. But is that not merely a matter of prudence? Of course, Nietzsche says. And the idea that has been touted by many philosophers, beginning with Plato, that on the one (lower) hand there is prudence, and on the other (exalted) hand morality, for which there are sanctions of a transcendental kind, strikes him as high-minded nonsense. So there is the level of morality at which it serves a useful function, and is required by any society that is to survive – though if you are powerful, of course you can get away with a great deal. But that only takes us as far as the continuance of life. What of giving life some point and purpose once we have got that far? The term 'morality' is often used to cover that too, though some people prefer to talk of 'ideals', which they say are essentially individual. Nietzsche does not investigate these matters of nomenclature, but when he is condemning morality or kinds of morality, and when he is calling himself an immoralist, he has the purpose and point of life in mind.

This is where things begin to get complicated. In trying to make them as clear as possible, I shall both depart to some extent from the chronological exposition of Nietzsche, and also rely very heavily on an article by Frithjof Bergmann, on 'Nietzsche's Critique of Morality' (Solomon and Higgins, 1988). But it should be reassuring that sometimes commentators agree – to the point of holding identical views. In the course of what I have to say, the distinction between morality as convenience and morality as ideal will virtually collapse, along with a good deal else.

The first thing to hold in mind is that Nietzsche does not deny the existence (in some sense) of values. It is a common and amazing mistake to think that he does. But the denial of value is what he primarily means by 'nihilism', the advent of which he dreads above all else. If he sometimes thinks of himself as the prophet of nihilism, it is not in the sense that he is proclaiming its arrival, as something to be celebrated, but in the sense that Jeremiah was the prophet of the destruction of Jerusalem. What he portrays, in book after book, is the gradual but accelerating decline of Western man into a state where no values any longer impress him, or where he mouths them but they mean nothing to him any longer. That is what he sees as imminent. How has this catastrophe, which none of his contemporaries seemed to recognize, come about, and how can it be remedied?

The answer involves looking at two aspects of morality. First, its grounding. Secondly, its content. Morality as it is still practised derives from the Hebraic–Christian tradition, in the largest measure, which means that its origins are to be found in the dictates of the god of a small Middle Eastern tribe, and that its contents remain very much what they were. That immediately transcendentalizes them in two ways. First, their deliverance is a matter of unquestionable commands, for which the punishment for violation was at one time instant divine retribution. Second, since the content was evidently designed for the continuance of the tribe, whose living conditions were vastly different in many ways from ours, it has had to be made more abstract and disconnected from the conditions in which we live. A result has been that morality has in part become unintelligible, and in part has to be coerced into relevance by making us into the kind of beings to whom it would sensibly apply, even though in many respects we know that that is false.

The matter is complicated further by the discrepancies between the Old and New Testaments, and Christ's disingenuousness in claiming that he had come not to destroy the law, but to fulfil it (Matt. 3: 17). Since many of his most impressive precepts are in sharp conflict with the Law, for instance 'Resist not evil', but the Old Testament has remained part of the canon of sacred texts, Christianity has always been in a state of moral identity-crisis. That, though a large factor in the moral bewilderment of the West, is a marginal issue for Nietzsche, whose main interest is in the nature of morality's sanctions in general.

For all sorts of reasons, philosophers of the last three hundred years or so have been concerned to stand by the moral precepts that they have inherited, while attempting to find new foundations for them, including the limiting case of denying that they need foundations. This being so, it is a pity that Nietzsche's Anglophobia led him to attack George Eliot when he was really attacking a tradition in which she plays an insignificant part. The attack comes in *Twilight of the Idols*, one of Nietzsche's last books, but it encapsulates, as so much of that witty and most trenchant of his works does, what he had been saying on the subject for a decade:

> They are rid of the Christian God and now believe all the more firmly that they must cling to Christian morality. That is an English consistency; we do not wish to hold it against little moralistic females à la Eliot. In England one must rehabilitate oneself after every little emancipation from theology by showing in a veritably awe-inspiring manner what a moral fanatic one is. That is the penance they pay there.

> We others hold otherwise. When one gives up the Christian faith, one pulls the right to Christian morality from under one's feet. This morality is by no means self-evident: this point has to be exhibited again and again, despite the English flatheads. Christianity is a system, a *whole* view of things thought out together. By breaking one main concept out of it, the faith in God, one breaks the whole: nothing necessary remains in one's hands. Christianity presupposes that man does not know, cannot know, what is good for him, what evil: he believes in God, who alone knows it. Christianity is a command; its origin is transcendent; it is beyond all criticism, all right to criticism; it has truth only if God is the truth – it stands and falls with faith in God.

> When the English actually believe that they know 'intuitively' what is good and evil, when they therefore suppose that they no longer require Christianity as the guarantee of morality, we merely witness the *effects* of the dominion of the Christian value-judgement and an expression of the strength and depth of this dominion: such that the origin of English morality has been forgotten, such that the very conditional character of

its right to existence is no longer felt. For the English, morality is not yet
a problem.

(TI, 'Skirmishes of an Untimely Man', 5)

Substitute for 'the English' 'the West' and this whole section seems to
me unanswerable. Yet apparently almost the only people to agree with
it are Christians, understandably insistent on their faith being seen as a
'system' (in some sense of the word). The most striking endorsement
of Nietzsche's argument here, the more impressive for having been
written in apparent ignorance of it, is G. E. M. Anscombe's famous
(among philosophers) paper 'Modern Moral Philosophy' (Thomson and
Dworkin, 1968). Writing as a traditional Roman Catholic, she says:

> the concepts of obligation, and duty – moral obligation and moral duty,
> that is to say – and of what is morally right and wrong, and of the moral
> sense of 'ought,' ought to be jettisoned if this is psychologically
> possible; because they are survivals, or derivatives from survivals, from
> an earlier conception of ethics which no longer generally survives, and
> are only harmful without it.

(Thomson and Dworkin, 1968: 186)

Needless to say, her proposal has not proved to be 'psychologically
possible', as she no doubt realized when she wrote those words. And
for the same reason that Nietzsche's claims have also been viewed as
'impossible', which is that we have no idea what to replace these terms
that 'ought to be jettisoned' with.

As one goes on reading Anscombe's article, one is amazed again and
again by the Nietzschean tone of this unwitting disciple. For example:

> To have a *law* conception of ethics is to hold that what is needed . . . is
> required by divine law . . . Naturally it is not possible to have such a
> conception unless you believe in God as a law-giver; like Jews, Stoics,
> and Christians . . . It is as if the notion 'criminal' were to remain when

criminal law and criminal courts had been abolished and forgotten.

(Thomson and Dworkin, 1968: 192–3)

Exactly so, and yet that, to Nietzsche's and Anscombe's dismay and contempt, is just how we do contrive to carry on, for the most part untroubled by the conceptual chaos involved, and hardly concealed.

Nietzsche, naturally, has a fundamentally different attitude to what this signifies in the long run, about man throughout history. In *Beyond Good and Evil*, written in 1885, he puts it in the widest context:

The strange narrowness of human evolution, its hesitations, its delays, its frequent retrogressions and rotations, are due to the fact that the herd instinct of obedience has been inherited best and at the expense of the art of commanding. If we think of this instinct taken to its ultimate extravagance there would be no commanders or independent men at all; or, if they existed, they would suffer from a bad conscience and in order to be able to command would have to practise a deceit upon themselves: the deceit, that is, that they too were only obeying. This state of affairs actually exists in Europe today: I call it the moral hypocrisy of the commanders. They know of no way of defending themselves against their bad conscience other than to pose as executors of more ancient or higher commands (commands of ancestors, of the constitution, of justice, of the law or even of God), or even to borrow herd maxims from the herd's way of thinking and appear as 'the first servant of the people' for example, or as 'instruments of the common good'. On the other hand, the herd-man in Europe today makes himself out to be the only permissible kind of man and glorifies the qualities through which he is tame, peaceable and useful to the herd as the real human virtues: namely public spirit, benevolence, consideration, industriousness, moderation, modesty, forbearance, pity. In those cases, however, in which leaders and bell-wethers are thought to be indispensable, there is attempt after attempt to substitute for them an adding-together of clever herd-men: this, for example, is the origin of all parliamentary constitutions. All this notwithstanding, what a blessing, what a release from a burden becoming intolerable, the appearance of an unconditional commander is for this herd-animal European, the effect produced by the appearance of Napoleon is the latest great witness – the history of the effect of Napoleon is almost the history of the higher happiness this entire century has attained in its most valuable men and moments.

(BGE 199)

This passage of Nietzsche at his most characteristic is likely to evoke mixed reactions. It moves between the highly persuasive, couched in his eloquent rhetorical-argumentative style, and the employment of terms which shock, still, as much as he must have intended that they should, even while they are bound to make most readers recoil from what he is saying. This use of the term 'herd-animal', and its cognates, is upsetting, as is the list of qualities which the 'herd-man' approves, for we approve them too: public-spiritedness, industriousness, modesty, and so on. And we approve them because we are herd-men, and are not at all convinced that we could become anything else, or whether if we could we would want to. And yet we have been made uneasy, since the whole issue of obedience has been raised, and while we are only too pleased to obey what we believe to be right, the question is why we have this belief, when we have abolished the commander – those of us who have. Of course, the fact that our moral convictions derive in the first place from the decrees of a god does not mean that, if the god is non-existent, the convictions are wrong. That is 'the fallacy of origins', a well-known and discredited device for discrediting beliefs. But on the other hand it would be foolish not to agree that if we have abandoned the original validating belief, we need something new in its place. For it is all too easy to be like 'the English' and think we know 'intuitively' what is right and wrong – it would be remarkable if we did, since we have no other substantial intuitive knowledge.

At this stage I don't want to look further into Nietzsche's specific views about the content of morality, except in so far as they are inseparable from his claims about the whole institution.

What he begins in *D* he carries on with tremendous panache in his next book, *The Gay Science*. It is here that he is more obviously preparing the ground for his breakthrough in values, which gets full-dress treatment in *Thus Spoke Zarathustra*. *GS* is his most refreshing book, in that he has the confidence in it to advance beyond the innumerable suggestions of his two previous books, while not yet bearing the prophetic weight that the authorship of *TSZ* put on him. And though the highly effective sniping of his so-called 'positivistic' period continues, one feels a more comprehensive grasp of what he is moving towards. The depth of the plight of post-Christian man is the most conspicuous feature of *GS*, which has, at section 125, the most famous of his announcements, that God is dead.

The section is entitled 'The Madman'. He is considered mad by all those in the market-place who hear him, because they have not the least idea what he is talking about. How could one kill God? It is the expression of Nietzsche's greatest anguish, since he sees as no one else does the consequences of God's death, sees what the long-term effect will be and is appalled at the thought of how people will behave once they have grasped the significance of God's no longer being the linchpin of their world. It does not matter – this is Nietzsche's gist – whether God existed or not. What makes the difference is whether we believe that He does. And over the course of centuries belief in God has eroded without people noticing what was happening. Its deepest consequence will be for values, because, as Nietzsche expresses it in an unpublished note: 'He who does not find greatness in God finds it nowhere. He must either deny it or create it.' And if we have the burden of creating greatness, then most of us, maybe all, will buckle under the weight. And without greatness life has no point, even if the greatness is beyond our reach. We shall explore later the dialectic by which Nietzsche traces God's demise to the inherently contradictory tendencies within Christianity itself. For the moment the important thing is that their result has occurred, that most people do not realize what it means, and that when they do they will no longer find life worth living.

Nietzsche's attitude to Christianity, like his attitude to most of the things he cared about, was divided at the deepest level. His contempt for the morality it inculcated has been sketched above, and it hardened as the years passed. But though he loathed the smallness of man that is part of Christian doctrine, and the set of virtues which are part of that, he was acutely aware of the achievements that only a Christian culture could have been responsible for. There will never be a Chartres built to celebrate humanist values, nor a Mass in B minor to affirm belief in them. So it looks as if the post-Christian era is most likely to be characterized by men who are smaller than the little Christians they have supplanted. Morality may be terrible, but what is it sensible to imagine replacing it?

Chapter 5
The One Thing Needful

The first four books of *GS* form a rising trajectory of brilliance and penetration. Book IV begins with a New Year's resolution which went the way that they nearly always do, but still marks the beginning of the surge of affirmation that led Nietzsche to *Thus Spoke Zarathustra*.

> I want to learn more and more to see as beautiful what is necessary in things; then I shall be one of those who make things beautiful. *Amor fati* (Love of fate): let that be my love henceforth! I do not want to wage war against what is ugly. I do not want to accuse; I do not want to accuse even those who accuse. *Looking away* shall be my only negation. And all in all and on the whole: some day I wish to be only a Yes-sayer
>
> (*GS* 276)

This passage of intense feeling is carried on in a way that can make one drunk, and it is perhaps unfair to look at it closely. That Nietzsche, our arch-diagnostician, could never look away, and that we would have lost much of his most valuable writing if he had, does something to mitigate the accusation that he never became only a Yes-sayer, and the fact that three of his last five books are attacks, two on Wagner and one on Christ, the only affirmative one being about himself.

For the time being, at least, his mood continues in this exalted way. Then, at section 290, we reach a point where he for the first time makes some clear suggestions as to the kind of people he hopes will replace the small men of late and post-Christianity:

> *One thing is needful.* – To 'give style' to one's character – a great and rare art! It is practised by those who survey all the strengths and weaknesses of their nature and then fit them into an artistic plan until every one of them appears as art and reason and even weaknesses delight the eye. Here a large mass of second nature has been added; there a piece of original nature has been removed – both times through long practice and daily work at it. Here the ugly that could not be removed is concealed; there it has been reinterpreted and made sublime. Much that is vague and resisted shaping has been saved and exploited for distant views; it is meant to beckon towards the far and immeasurable. In the end, when the work is finished, it becomes evident how the constraint of a single taste governed and formed everything large and small. Whether this taste was good or bad is less important than one might suppose, if only it was a single taste!
>
> (GS 290)

That is not the whole section, but it is enough to be going on with.

The idea that we might become 'artists of life' had been mooted in *BT*, but in a context so different as to make the idea of a continuity specious. What Nietzsche is starting on the road to advocating in *GS* is an extreme individualism, within a framework that does not lead to a scarcely intelligible atomism. But as soon as we are impressed by his vision, we start to wonder too. For the analogy with art, or the art of landscape gardening, which is adumbrated here is clearly one that cannot be worked through straightforwardly. One only lives once (I shall be dealing later with the Eternal Recurrence, which is anyway not going to help here: mistakes made this time round have been, and will be, repeated infinitely). But the artist, with rare exceptions, can tinker with his works indefinitely until he feels that he has got things as right as he ever will. What Nietzsche is proposing is that we carry out a scrupulous survey of our character, assessing it, though we are not told at this stage by what criteria – what are to count as strengths and weaknesses – and give it that unity which is what is called having style. Fitting the elements of our make-up into 'an artistic plan' does rather give the impression that we are less subject to outside contingencies than anyone but a hermit is bound to be.

Despite these preliminary doubts, there is something enticing about Nietzsche's suggestion. It inaugurates his new form of Classicism, where 'it will be the strongest and most domineering natures that enjoy their finest gaiety in such constraint and perfection under a law of their own', as opposed to 'the weak characters without power over themselves that hate the constraint of style' (i.e. Romantics). And although Nietzsche makes a lot of the idea of individual style, it is evident that he is appealing to a notion of style which exists apart from the individual; if there were not some external criteria then anyone would have style as long as he was distinguishable from other people. The mere use of the concept of style is enough to make us think of given frameworks within which people work, achieving individuality thanks to the support which the framework offers. An obvious case is the Classical Style in music, as manifest from Haydn through Mozart and Beethoven, petering out at some indeterminate point. The constraints of that style were rigorous, but one cannot imagine any one of those three composers thriving without it. They were able to be themselves because so much was already given. It is in the tension between the style which was available to anyone at the time, and which we can see working perfectly satisfactorily without producing works of genius in the hands of, say, Hummel, who owes it entirely to the style available to him that he can be worthwhile at all, and the strongly defined individualities of its great masters that we locate its supreme achievements.

But, the whole drift of Nietzsche's analysis of culture runs, that was then, and now is quite different. There is no longer a common style with which to work in creative tension, so we have to find our own. Clearly in such circumstances the very notion of style is severely strained. The fact that he says that 'Whether this taste was good or bad is less important than one might suppose, if only it was a single taste!' implies that the criteria he is employing here are not only aesthetic but also formal. The nature of the elements takes second place to their configuration. That may make us wonder, again, about whether it matters what the elements are at all, and surely Nietzsche thought that it did. At the end of the section he writes: 'For one thing is needful: that a human being should attain satisfaction with himself, whether it be by means of this or that poetry or art; only then is a human being at all tolerable to behold'. But attaining satisfaction with oneself can at best be a necessary condition. There are plenty of people who have attained satisfaction with themselves who are intolerable to behold, and for that very reason.

Such passages as this do raise the question of how far one should press Nietzsche. For all his own tendencies to extremes and exaggerations of expression, he somehow manages to exercise tact, by not pressing in inappropriate places. But the opposite danger is that we call him 'stimulating', which means that we do not take seriously what he says. In this particular case, some tactlessness may be worth risking, because it does contain in embryo thoughts that will be central to his work, but they will be so much more portentous than he is here that it may be better to see him in his human rather than his superhuman dimensions.

So, while leaving open the matter of whether he is giving the man of style *carte blanche* on the issue of the elements of his character, we can agree that one of the things about a person which leads us to say that he has style is his capacity to carry things off, to incorporate disparate and what for most people would be embarrassing or humiliating experiences and make them part of a larger scheme. There is a moving, funny, and memorable moment at the end of Jean Renoir's film *La*

Règle du jeu in which, after a shocking shooting incident in which a flying ace is killed during a country-house holiday, the host speaks to the stunned assembled guests with such exquisite taste and carefully chosen words that one of the guests says to another 'He called it an accident. A new definition!' But he receives a rebuke: 'He has style, and that's a rare thing these days'. Quite so. The elegant speech has preserved decorum, kept what is evidently a precarious civilized façade in place, and sent the guests to bed in elegiac rather than recriminatory or inchoate mood. There is strength in such capacity for what may seem like euphemism, the strength to cope with what are, for any complex person, experiences which could lead to disintegration or at the very least self-loathing.

Nietzsche is candid about what is involved. A few sections later he asks

Nietzsche

> How can we make things beautiful, attractive and desirable for us when they are not? And I rather think that in themselves they never are . . . Moving away from things until there is a good deal that one no longer sees . . . all this we should learn from artists while being wiser than they are in other matters. For with them this subtle power usually comes to an end where art ends and life begins; but we want to be the poets of our life – first of all in the smallest, most everyday matters.
>
> (*GS* 299)

In other, less tactful and tasteful, words: do not be too scrupulous with yourself about getting things right, that is, true. It is more important that you should make them tolerable at least, beautiful at best.

I suspect that what Nietzsche has in mind is something more instinctive than what he gives the impression of recommending – inevitably, since he has to spell out what he would like us already to know and act on. It is a dilemma he finds himself in over and over again – should he content himself with dropping hints, or should he say what he thinks it is necessary for us to know in skywriting? He

48

wants us to be the kind of people who only need hints because we are so fine-tuned, but he knows that we will be deaf to anything less than apocalyptic thunder – and then accuse him of making too much noise. At the stage of *GS* he still tries allusive, tantalizing formulas, leaving us to make the connections between them. The weariness that Zarathustra will often suffer, as he realizes that he is always going to be misunderstood, has not yet begun to afflict him. And he is not sure, either, whether one can only educate people in taste if they are merely ignorant, or if it is possible to re-educate those whose taste is already formed, and corrupt. *GS* is, fundamentally, the book of an optimist – the last that Nietzsche could conscientiously write.

At any rate, this is the relatively relaxed side of Nietzsche, as opposed to what J. P. Stern has justly called 'the moralist of strenuousness'. For if any hint of effort appears in someone's character – if it seems that they are willing their charm, warmth, serenity, at-homeness with themselves – then that is a crucial failure of style. Yet in our hideous freedom from the welcome constraints of tradition, and given the correspondingly large number of ways of living that *seem* to be open to us, far too many of which actually are, we are unlikely to be able to organize 'the chaos within us' without some visible signs of strain. Even Goethe, who comes increasingly to represent Nietzsche's ideal of self-organization, was unable to conceal the effort it cost. He was, of course, a limiting case of unity imposed on diversity, a diversity of interests and impulses that would leave most of us paralysed.

Nietzsche's claim that giving one's character style is 'the one thing needful' (a phrase which is probably intended to parody Wagner, whose chief figures are typically preoccupied with an overriding need) has an unexpected bearing on his critique of pity, one of the most notorious of his insistences, and one of the most consistently maintained. In one of his incredibly brilliant pieces of prose, unfortunately too long to quote in full, he considers 'the will to suffer and those who feel pity'. He asks whether it is good for either the pitier or his object to be in that relationship, and shows in the sensitive discussion that follows that his aversion to pity is nothing to do, at any rate in the way normally taken, with being heartless or ruthless or unfeeling. So far as the pitied person is concerned, he points out that the economy of his soul-states is a delicate affair, that those who notice that he is in distress and therefore hurry to help 'assume the role of fate', and that it never occurs to them that the sufferer may need his anguish, which is intertwined with his joy; 'No, the "religion of pity" (or "the heart") commands them to help, and they believe that they have helped most when they have helped most quickly' (GS 338).

It is clear that Nietzsche is not talking about giving a starving person food and drink, or administering anaesthetics to someone about to undergo an operation. His attack is concerned with pity as a full-time occupation of sorting out people's lives, with a noble neglect, as we are taught, of one's own interests. So it is merely vulgar (and very common indeed) to misinterpret him as advocating neglect of others' basic requirements, as his immediately following discussion of the effects of pity on the pitier makes plain. 'I know, there are a hundred decent and praiseworthy ways of losing my own way, and they are truly highly "moral"! Indeed, those who now preach the morality of pity even take the view that this and only this is moral – to lose one's own way in order to come to the assistance of a neighbour' (GS 338). And he continues eloquently to stress how hard, often how lonely and remote from gratitude and warmth the pursuit of one's own way is. He concludes, tellingly, with 'my morality which says to me: Live in seclusion so that you can live for yourself.'

Many people will feel that a morality which insists on their following their own way is one which they simply cannot follow, for the obvious reason that they do not have 'a way' – they have competences, needs, anxieties, and problems, but nothing that for them is an individuating goal. In suggesting that each person becomes the artist of his own life, Nietzsche is probably operating with the rather exigent view we now have, or had until very recently, of what constitutes a work of art, originality ranking high among its desirable, or even its necessary, qualities. And that seems just absurd as a wish about human beings, let alone an injunction; it presupposes that most people have it in them to be unique in a fairly strong sense, an assumption that, if he held it, Nietzsche should certainly have given prominence to.

In fact he is thinking of, at the lowest, those people who can read him with understanding – not that he says that, so far as I am aware; but if one could not do that, the chances of summoning up the kinds of energies required for following 'one's own way' would be nugatory. That already limits the number of people he is talking about to a tiny proportion of the population. What about the rest? How can he condemn herd-men when they have no capacity for being anything else? But he does not condemn them; he is simply not interested in them. That raises the whole issue of his politics, or lack of them, which gives rise to more canting among commentators than any other single feature of his thought. I shall deal with it later. But what about people who can read him with understanding but still feel that there is no special way that is theirs? Is it Nietzsche's view that they are deluding themselves in order to have an easy time of it, or that they may be right? If the first, he seems to be holding a rather surprising, for him, estimate of the possibilities of people. If the second, then what he says about giving one's life style is irrelevant, and one may wonder what they are supposed to do with themselves – those gifted, intelligent, cultivated, sensitive, receptive people who have no inclination to develop a high profile, because despite their gifts they are essentially passive. Or is no one essentially passive? More questions for later in the agenda.

One other outstanding question needs to be looked at before we leave the matter of style, endlessly discussable as it is. One of the finest of Nietzsche's commentators, Alexander Nehamas, has raised it (Nehamas, 1985) and failed to come up with a remotely satisfactory answer. It is this: Can someone who has, by standards that one can imagine few rejecting, certainly not Nietzsche, a wholly deplorable character still pass his tests for having style? If Nietzsche's criteria were purely formal, that is, all the bits fit together and it does not matter what they are individually, then the appalling answer would seem to be yes. Nehamas writes 'I think that there is something admirable in the very fact of having character or style' (Nehamas, 1985: 192). What about Goering? His style is undeniable and unmistakable, but one hopes he has few admirers. Nehamas:

> It is not clear to me whether a consistently and irredeemably vicious person does actually have a character; the sort of agent Aristotle describes as 'bestial' probably does not. In some way there is something inherently praiseworthy in having character or style that prevents extreme cases of vice from being praised even in Nietzsche's formal sense.
>
> (Nehamas, 1985: 193)

This is embarrassing: the only way Nehamas could push through his claim would be by blatant linguistic stipulation, which is what this passage comes to.

It is not necessary to wriggle like this on Nietzsche's behalf. As I said, what he proposes in *GS* is to be taken as preliminary moves towards a goal of which he was not yet at all confident. He is bracing himself for his *chef d'œuvre*, and the last two sections of Book IV, the end of the first edition of *GS*, are pregnant with the book on which he staked his fame. The penultimate section, 'The greatest weight', introduces the notion of the Eternal Recurrence, as an idea too horrifying for any but the strongest to bear. But those who are the strongest will exult in it. Then the final section, 'Incipit tragoedia', is almost word for word the same as the opening of *Thus Spoke Zarathustra*, a trailer for that work, and unintelligible except in that capacity. It is, one must concede, Nietzsche's least subtle effort to give his life's work a unity.

Chapter 6
Prophecy

For a long time Nietzsche's most famous book was *Thus Spoke Zarathustra*. It is not, I think, any longer, and on the whole that is a development I applaud. Written in short bursts of inspiration, it shows all too clearly the worst signs of that state, though it also contains some of his best writing. What Nietzsche was trying to do in it was to establish himself as a philosopher-poet, and for that purpose he employed a set of idioms that reveal dismayingly what his idea of poetry was. He uses a great deal of imagery and allegory, but he does that elsewhere too, and to much better effect. One's initial impression is of pastiche: most obviously biblical pastiche, ranging from straightforward echoes of the Bible to parody – the range of moods is easily overlooked by the reader somewhat numbed by the reiteration of 'Thus spoke Zarathustra' at the end of each section. There are poems, some of which have become famous, and have been employed by many composers, of whom the most successful have been Mahler and Delius. One can see why the poems should have had the appeal they did for those two composers in particular, men of extraordinarily strong will-power who spent much of their time evoking the earth in its fullness and beauty, enduring, in contrast with the poignant brevity of human life. But their success betrays an element in Nietzsche–Zarathustra which he was at pains to disown: nostalgia.

The most genuine tone of *TSZ*, which surfaces in surprising places, is one of regret. The least convincing tone is of exaltation and affirmation, the qualities that Zarathustra is at such pains to inculcate, since they are necessary to prepare the ground for the arrival of the *Übermensch*, whose prophet Zarathustra is. But he is a prophet who is intent on not having disciples, a desire which he is keen to stress, since it singles him out from all other prophets. But one might ask whether someone who speaks the truth should not want disciples, as many as possible. The answer would seem to be that Zarathustra is not at all sure of the truth which impels him to leave his mountain and to 'go down' or 'go under' – a carefully calculated ambiguity on Nietzsche's part. The magician in Part IV gives voice to the melancholy that is Zarathustra's constant companion, when he sings '*That I be banished from all truth, Only fool! Only poet!*' Again, in the last section of Part I, 'On the gift-giving virtue', Zarathustra speaks to his disciples in words that Nietzsche was so proud of that he quotes them at the end of the Foreword to *Ecce Homo*:

> Truly, I counsel you: go away from me and resist Zarathustra! And even better: be ashamed of him! Perhaps he deceived you . . . One repays a teacher badly if one always wants to remain nothing but a pupil. And why do you not want to pluck at my wreath? . . . you say you believe in Zarathustra? But what matters Zarathustra? You are my believers – but what matter all believers? You had not yet sought yourselves: and you found me. Thus do all believers; therefore all faith amounts to little.

It is a powerful passage, but for all its ponderable wisdom it is strange coming from a prophet. For prophets do not argue, they announce. And so by what methods are the disciples to discover what is true and what false in Zarathustra's teaching? The refusal to accept homage that is not justified by independent checks on the truth is admirable, and clearly meant as part of Nietzsche's running battle with Christ. But it leaves us in the dark as to how to cope with Zarathustra's teaching, for decadent as we are, we are not in the best position to criticize.

The trouble with a self-doubting prophet, one who advises caution as to anything he says, is bad enough: we are in the presence of an incarnate oxymoron. But the dangers of being a poet, to which Zarathustra is not the first to alert us, only compound the problem of how to deal with a philosopher-artist, who seems more than incrementally suspect. All we can do, under these inauspicious conditions, is to try to share Zarathustra's visions, and see to what extent they command our imaginations, always remembering that those are corrupt. But then if it turns out that the vision itself is vague and opaque, we shall have to do what in the end I am convinced is the only thing that one really can do with the book, which is to savour it in a picaresque way.

There are enough wonderful things, despite all the caveats I have depressingly entered, to make reading it a memorable experience. It begins impressively, with Zarathustra's descent from his mountain, and what one might call his Sermon off the Mount is written with genuine inspiration. But Zarathustra soon gets on to his central theme: 'Behold, I teach you the *Übermensch*. The *Übermensch is* the meaning of the earth. Let your will say: the *Übermensch* shall be the meaning of the earth! I beseech you, my brothers, *remain faithful to the earth*, and do not believe those who speak to you of otherworldly hopes!' (*TSZ* I, Prologue, 3). That introduces the first of Zarathustra's three major concepts. And his injunction to be faithful to the earth is one of Nietzsche's great recurring themes, and one with which I feel the greatest sympathy. But what we now wait for is some illumination about how the *Übermensch* is the meaning of the earth, what steps might be taken to bring about his arrival, and what he will be like when he appears. Unfortunately we get very little information about any of these matters. There are crude misunderstandings which can be quickly cleared up, such as that the *Übermensch* would be an evolutionary phenomenon. There is no reason to think that he will not be human in form, but that is minimally enlightening. He seems to be defined in large part in terms of the second of Zarathustra's announcements, that of the Eternal Recurrence. The *übermensch is* the being who can joyfully embrace that doctrine, for doctrine, or dogma, is what it is. And the third of Zarathustra's teachings is the Will to Power, the fundamental reality of existence. Once more, the *Übermensch* manifests it in its purest, most impressive way: as self-overcoming, whatever that comes to.

One of the things it comes to is made clear during the course of Zarathustra's progress. Zarathustra, it may be worth pointing out, is the herald of the *Übermensch* but is not himself one. Yet they share many characteristics, and it seems often that the best handle we can get on the *Übermensch is* that he is a heightened version of Zarathustra.

When, for instance, in Part IV, the soothsayer tells Zarathustra what his final sin is, it turns out to be pity for man. The *Übermensch*, one takes it, would realize without being tempted that this is the ultimate seduction. He would be able to accept that man suffers, but it would not make him suffer – and to what point, if he did? We have been so infused with suffering, and with the view that it is the most ineradicable element in existence, as indeed for us it is, that we take it that in some way it is the deepest state there is. Because joy is always ephemeral, we regard it as superficial too – or that is the temptation. The only joy we have heard about that is eternal is the joy of the next world, which we have no grasp of. For understandable biological reasons, we regard joy, or pleasure, as the terminus of a process and thus as displaced as soon as the next process, or the next stage of the same process, begins. To that extent we are all modified Schopenhauerians, Schopenhauer having taken the more extreme line that pleasure is *nothing* more than the temporary cessation of pain. By this stage in his career, Nietzsche was wholly opposed to Schopenhauer, who is, along with his former idol Wagner, one of the gallery of more or less ludicrous figures thinly disguised in *TSZ*. It is Zarathustra's teaching – and does he want his disciples to disagree? – that joy is deeper than suffering, as we learn in the chapter in Part IV called 'The Drunken Song' (that, at any rate, is how it appears in the English translations; the German in the new Critical Edition is '*Das Nachtwandlers-Lied*' – 'The Sleep-walker's Song'):

> The world is deep,
> Deeper than day had been aware. Deep is its woe;
> Joy – deeper yet than agony:
> Woe implores: Go!
> But all joy wills eternity –
> Wills deep, wills deep eternity.

It is not, even in German, distinguished poetry. But its basic sentiment is moving, and has, for Zarathustra, the closest connection with the Eternal Recurrence. Earlier in the same section Zarathustra had made that clear:

> Have you ever said Yes to a single joy? O my friends, then you said Yes too to *all* woe. All things are entangled, ensnared, enamoured; if ever you wanted one thing twice, if ever you said, 'You please me, happiness! Abide, moment!' then you wanted *all* back. All anew, all eternally, all entangled, ensnared, enamoured – oh, then you *loved* the world. Eternal ones, love it eternally and evermore; and to woe too, you say: go, but return! For *all joy wills eternity*.

This is Nietzsche's lyrical, not to say gushing, version of his elsewhere more austerely expressed view that saying Yes to anything is saying Yes to everything, since the causal network is such that any state depends on the rest of Nature being in the condition it is. That is, at least initially, the view of the Eternal Recurrence that he promulgates. The *Übermensch is* the being who is prepared to say Yes to whatever comes along, because joy and sorrow are, as always for Nietzsche, from the Primal Oneness of *BT* onwards, inseparable. So despite the horror of existence up to now, he is prepared to affirm it all. That, at any rate, is how I understand it, and him.

But that is only the beginning of an account of *übermenschlichkeit*. For having expressed his unconditional acceptance of existence to the point where he wills that everything should be repeated, exactly as it has been, in eternal cycles, there still remains the question of what the *Übermensch* does with his time. Something, presumably, very different from man, who is defined early on as a rope, tied between beast and *Übermensch* – a rope over an abyss' (*TSZ* I, Prologue, 4). He will be as different from us as we are from the beasts. Whatever he does will be done in a mood of affirmation, but what will it be? We know what it will not be – anything small, reactive, resentful. There is a strain of antinomianism in Zarathustra which suggests that if you have the right basic attitude you can do what you like. That comes out clearly in the chapter entitled 'On Chastity', where he says

> Do I counsel you to slay your senses? I counsel the innocence of the senses. Do I counsel you to chastity? Chastity is a virtue in some, but almost a vice in many. They abstain, but the bitch sensuality leers enviously out of everything they do. even to the heights of their virtue and to the cold regions of the spirit this beast follows them with her lack of peace. And how nicely the bitch sensuality knows how to beg for a piece of spirit when denied a piece of meat.

There is a touch of puritanism there, but it is shrewd, especially the last sentence, and in the generally imperative tone of *TSZ* it comes as a relief. But there is a dominant line, apart from tone, which leads in the opposite direction – not one of repressiveness, but a stress on arduousness and hardness, above all with oneself. That is what we would expect, given that Nietzsche's primary concern is with greatness; and comfort, satisfaction, sensual gratification are inimical to greatness. In what way will the *Übermensch* be great? Nietzsche always has at least one eye on artistic achievement, so one might expect stupendous works of art from him, but on that subject *TSZ* is strangely silent. It is, of course, fruitless to meditate on works of art that have not yet been created, as it is not to dwell on scientific achievements still to be realized, since in the latter case we know what it is we want answers to. But in art there are no questions in that sense. Furthermore, the idea of a group of *Übermenschen* all being artists does seem ridiculous. But then what will they be? It is no good speculating further because Nietzsche provides us with no clues on the subject. Indeed, it seems that he was unable to make any progress with it, and although he is as famous for coining the term as for anything else, it does not occur again in his work, except in the self-celebrations of *Ecce Homo*, where he goes on about *TSZ* much longer than about any of his other books, saying 'Here man is overcome at every moment, the concept *Übermensch* here becomes the greatest reality' (*EH*, 'Thus Spoke Zarathustra', 6).

But that is a sad piece of wishful thinking. Nietzsche has succumbed to the besetting temptation of creators of ideals – the ideal is so far removed from the squalidly real that all that can be done is to dwell on the ghastliness of reality and say that the ideal is nothing like that. One is reminded of Swift's portrayal, in *Gulliver's Travels*, of the disgusting Yahoos (us) and the approvable Houyhnhnms, about whom Leavis justly remarked that 'they may have all the reason, but the Yahoos have all the life . . . The clean skin of the Houyhnhnms, in short, is stretched over a void; instincts, emotions and life, which complicate the problem of cleanliness and decency, are left for the Yahoos with the dirt and the indecorum.' There is an uncanny resemblance here to man and *Übermensch*, though perhaps it is not so surprising, given the difficulties that anyone trying to indicate an ideal that transcends and negates humanity is bound to encounter.

Early on in *TSZ* there is an alternative, or maybe it is meant as a complementary account of the progress of what is there called 'the spirit'. It is the first of Zarathustra's Speeches, at which stage he still seems uneasy with figurative language, to judge from the clumsiness of this passage, which induces, as Erich Heller remarks, 'a sense of extreme zoological and spiritual discomfort' (Heller, 1988: 71). The spirit here begins as a camel, that is to say modern man, weighed down by the accumulation of the values it has to bear, a whole oppressive tradition of obligations and the guilt attendant on their inevitable violation. Speeding off into the desert, the camel staggers; but finally revolts and metamorphoses into a lion, with the intention of fighting a dragon. The dragon is named 'Thou shalt' and is thus the creator of the camel's intolerable burden. It claims that 'All value has long been created, and I am all created value.' The lion resists, intent on replacing 'Thou shalt' with 'I will'. But though the lion can fight, all he can create is the freedom for new values; he cannot create the values themselves. He says a sacred 'No', and that is the end of him – he has served the only purpose he can. So far so clear. The last transformation is a surprise: for it is a child.

> Why must the preying lion still become a child? The child is innocence and forgetting, a new beginning, a game, a self-propelled wheel, a first movement, a sacred 'Yes'. For the game of creation, my brothers, a sacred 'Yes' is needed: the spirit now wills his own will, and he who had been lost to the world now conquers his own world.

This must be, among other things, Nietzsche's version of Christ's 'Except ye become as little children, ye shall not enter into the kingdom of heaven' (Matt. 18: 18). And elsewhere Nietzsche uses the phrase 'the innocence of becoming'. At moments of stress in his writing, he sometimes resorts to formulations which are oxymoronic or in the deepest sense sentimental, because he knows that one element in the combination is too deeply embedded in us to be withdrawn, while the other is what would redeem it, despite its manifest incompatibility. Thus as early as *BT* we hear of 'a Socrates who practises music', whereas it is of the essence of the Socrates that Nietzsche has idiosyncratically portrayed that he is anti-musical. And in an unpublished note he writes of 'the Roman Caesar with Christ's soul'.

Are these merely touching attempts to square the circle, or can they be forced to mean something? There are good reasons for saying the former, because Nietzsche was a desperately divided man. He could not help admiring far more about Socrates than he officially should; and as we shall see, *The Antichrist* gets almost out of control as his portrayal of the alleged 'ideal decadent' takes lyrical wings. And, to return to *TSZ*, his general attitude to life is what video libraries call 'highly adult', yet he is entranced by the thought of a child wholly absorbed in play, serious and rapt, innocent but also ignorant. Can he have wanted his *Übermensch* to be like Wagner's Siegfried, brought up with no knowledge of the world – and coming to grief for want of it? It seems unlikely. That phrase 'a new beginning' is dangerous. For it is usually Nietzsche's distinction as a connoisseur of decadence to realize that among our options is not that of wiping the slate clean. We need to have a self to overcome, and that self will be the result of the whole Western tradition, which it will somehow manage to 'aufheben', a word that Nietzsche has no fondness for, because of its virtual Hegelian copyright, and which means simultaneously 'to obliterate', 'to preserve' and 'to lift up'. Isn't that just what the *Übermensch* is called upon to do, or if we drop him, what we, advancing from our present state, must do if we are to be 'redeemed'? The ideal of being a child, or as a child, has, apart from its Christian affiliations, Romantic ones which it is strange to see Nietzsche endorsing. The element which he wants to stress, I am sure, is the unselfconsciousness that young children possess. But for us, or an advance on us, to achieve that now is hardly imaginable.

So we are back with the *Übermensch* as embracing the Eternal Recurrence. And that has proved the most riddling of all Nietzsche's views. Is it meant simply in a 'What if . . . ?' spirit, or as a serious hypothesis about the nature of the cosmos? In the penultimate section of Book IV of *GS* it is certainly the former. But in his notebooks, including especially those that were posthumously edited as *The Will to Power*, he tries giving proofs of it as a general theory, based on the fact that if the number of atoms in the universe is finite, they must reach a configuration that they have been in before, and that will inevitably result in the history of the universe repeating itself. This is one of the least rewarding areas of his speculation, and his failure to publish these experimental thoughts is a cause for rejoicing – or would be if scholars were not intent on scanning them for clues to what he really thought. They are encouraged by his own excitement at the idea, which occurred to him in the Swiss Engadine, 'six thousand feet above man and time' and which he regarded, evidently, as one of those intuitions in which one is convinced that there is something deep and true, though one cannot say precisely what it is.

The cosmological view of the doctrine has not in general been regarded favourably. Yet commentators are so impressed by Niezsche's own enthusiasm for the doctrine, or at any rate its name, that they use their ingenuity to explain what he really meant by it. I can only say here that in trying to render it intelligible and interesting what they produce makes one wonder why Nietzsche should have given it so misleading a nomenclature. Tersely: if by 'Eternal Recurrence' he did not mean Eternal Recurrence, why did he not call it what he did mean?

So we are left with the 'What if . . . ?' approach. My initial reaction was to say that I would not give a damn, thus surprisingly qualifying for *übermenschlich* status, on the verificationist ground that if each cycle is, as it has to be, precisely the same as the previous and successive ones, then we have no knowledge of what happened, and especially not of what we did, last time round, so can neither take steps to avoid the consequences of what was disastrous, nor think with horror or joy of what lies ahead. If the Eternal Recurrence were true, this would be the nth time I was writing this book, but that would do nothing to lead me to alter its contents. That would seem to be that. But for many people with whom I have discussed the idea, though they agree that it can make no difference to anything, they are still reluctant to say that it has no effect on how they feel about things. As someone asked me recently: which is worse, a universe in which Auschwitz occurs once, or one in which it occurs infinitely many times? It seems to need, to say the least, an unfeeling person to say that it does not matter. Recurrence, even if it makes, in practical terms, no difference, still invests with a terrible weight what *does* happen.

Kundera, in what has now become a rather famous passage at the beginning of his novel *The Unbearable Lightness of Being*, has this as the core of his brief but pregnant thoughts on the subject:

> Let us therefore agree that the idea of eternal return implies a perspective from which things appear other than as we know them: they appear without the mitigating circumstance of their transitory nature. This mitigating circumstance prevents us from coming to a verdict. For how can we condemn something that is ephemeral, in transit? In the sunset of dissolution, everything is illuminated by the aura of nostalgia, even the guillotine

(Kundera, 1984: 4)

The key, or give-away clause there, is the first one. The reason why people's imaginations are so gripped by the idea is that they take up a perspective outside any one cycle, so that they can visualize it occurring again and again. It may perhaps even be the shift from seeing oneself as locked in the cycle, and viewing the whole thing from a god's-eye point of view, that generates the thrill, and the sense of intolerable weight, or, if one is an arch-yes-sayer, the rapture of return.

I remain a sceptic; it does nothing for me either way, though I can appreciate the inspiration that it has given great artists, such as Yeats in his 'A Dialogue of Self and Soul':

> I am content to live it all again,
> and yet again . . .
> I am content to follow to its source
> Every event in action or in thought;

> Measure the lot; forgive myself the lot!
>
> When such as I cast out remorse
>
> So great a sweetness flows into the breast
>
> We must laugh and we must sing,
>
> We are blest by everything,
>
> Everything we look upon is blest.

Those lines, inconceivable if Yeats had not read and been profoundly impressed by Nietzsche, are also a good example of how he can influence people who have only a vague and inaccurate idea of what he is saying – something one sometimes suspects of Nietzsche himself. And they contain much that Nietzsche is most ardent in his advocacy of, most particularly the idea of casting out remorse. But he arrives at that view in his later writings not via Eternal Recurrence, but through penetrating psychological analyses of the effects of remorse and backwards-looking in general.

There is one further line on the Eternal Recurrence which is worth mentioning briefly, because it renders it something of a joke, though by no stretch of the imagination does it count among Nietzsche's best. That is that it is a parody of all doctrines of another world whose relationship to this one – this 'preposterous, pragmatical pig of a world', to quote Yeats again – is one of ontological and axiological superiority. Instead of heaven and hell, or the world of unchanging Platonic forms, it suggests this world made eternal through meaningless repetition. Whereas other-worldly doctrines allege that this world only gains value through being related to another world, the Eternal Recurrence teasingly suggests that this world is deprived of value by a process analogous to that whereby a sentence is repeated until it becomes nothing more than a series of noises. To return to Kundera: weight is attached to incidents by the thought that they happen more than once, whereas 'Einmal ist keinmal' ('Once is nothing', or better: 'Try anything twice'); but weight is one thing, value another. Kundera, in this respect a faithful disciple of

Nietzsche, manages a nimble dialectic between lightness and heaviness, meaning or value and futility. Do we, should we, does it make sense to ask whether we should, value something more on account of its uniqueness or because it is representative, at the limit of an infinite series? The shortest answer is that it depends on what your temperament is. Nietzsche, with his all-too-protean temperament, was inclined to answer 'Both' and also 'Neither'.

The third of Zarathustra's cardinal teachings is that of the Will to Power. It gets its first mention in the chapter in the Part I called 'On the Thousand and One Goals', which recounts how Zarathustra visited many nations, finding that each needed to esteem, but something different from their neighbour. And then:

> A tablet of the good hangs over every people. Behold, it is the tablet of their overcomings; behold, it is the voice of their will to power. Praiseworthy is whatever seems difficult to a people; whatever seems indispensable and difficult is called good; and whatever liberates even out of the deepest need, the rarest, the most difficult – that they call holy.

And later in the same chapter, stressing the connection of power with value: 'To esteem is to create: hear this, you creators! Esteeming itself is of all esteemed things the most estimable treasure. Through esteeming alone is there value: and without esteeming, the nut of existence would be hollow'. But at the end of the chapter he says 'Humanity still has no goal. But tell me, my brothers, if humanity still lacks a goal – is humanity itself not still lacking too?' How the will to power is tied in with valuing is better discussed later. That is still clearer from the other brief mention of the will to power, in the chapter in Part II called 'On Self-Overcoming'. There Zarathustra says 'Indeed, the truth was not hit by him who shot at it with the word of the "will to existence": that will does not exist [a swipe at Schopenhauer] . . .

Only where there is life is there also will: not will to life but – thus I teach you – will to power.'

And that is virtually all that Nietzsche says on the subject in *TSZ*. Once more we find, in other words, that Zarathustra is a prophet more of what his author will be writing later than of anything worked out and seriously discussable. His problem is that he is resolutely opposed to systems and system-builders, as many remarks show. But it is not clear how he can avoid a system if he is to promulgate a new table of values. This dilemma leads him to make the worst of both worlds: he drops tantalizing hints, which lay him open to multiple interpretations and misunderstandings. But though the hints imply a huge submerged richness of thought, we are denied that and told that we must disagree, if we can, with thoughts expressed too fragmentarily for us even to know what to disagree with. That is the harshest estimate of *TSZ*. Much less harsh ones are defensible. But I prefer to move on to his post-Zarathustra works, where his powers are at their height, and he does not have to cope with looking dignified in his prophetic mantle.

Nietzsche

Chapter 7
Occupying the High Ground

Thus Spoke Zarathustra was written in the aftermath of the single most devastating experience of Nietzsche's life: his rejection by Lou Salomé, to whom he proposed marriage through his friend Paul Rée, only to discover that they were closer to one another than they were to him. Lou was an immensely gifted woman, who went on to become Rilke's mistress and later one of Freud's most valued disciples; he pays tribute to her in uncharacteristically generous terms for her discoveries in the area of anal eroticism. Nietzsche briefly envisaged a partnership in which he could carry on his work, understood and aided by a woman whom he could regard as an equal. There is a bizarre photograph, taken at his insistence, in which he and Rée are drawing an ox-cart, while Lou stands in it brandishing a whip over them. It provides an unexpected slant – whether or not the connection ever occurred to Nietzsche is immaterial – on that notorious remark in *TSZ*, when an old woman says to Zarathustra 'Are you going to a woman? Do not forget your whip!'

The rejection humiliated Nietzsche to the point of utter despair. Writing to one of his closest friends, Franz Overbeck on Christmas Day 1882, he says:

> This last *morsel of life* was the hardest I have yet had to chew, and it is still possible that I shall *choke* on it. I have suffered from the humiliating

and tormenting memories of this summer as from a bout of madness –
what I indicated in Basle and in my last letter concealed the most
essential thing. It involves a tension between opposing passions which I
cannot cope with. That is to say, I am exerting every ounce of my self-
mastery; but I have lived in solitude too long and fed too long off my
'own fat,' so that I am now being broken, as no other man could be, on
the wheel of my own passions . . . Unless I discover the alchemical trick
of turning this – muck into gold, I am lost. Here I have the most
beautiful chance to prove that for me 'all experiences are useful, all
days holy and all people divine'!!!

(Middleton, 1969: 198–9; the passage in inverted commas is from the
epigraph to the first edition of *GS*, derived from Emerson.)

It was on that basis that he set about writing *TSZ*, and his agonies
doubtless contributed to the exalted mode which sometimes makes
the book hard to bear. But given his disappointment and his loneliness,
the effort to perform the alchemist's trick is impressively successful.
His torments are probably responsible, too, for the equivocal tone of
much of *TSZ*, which I paid no attention to in my remarks on it. But
Zarathustra is prone to depressions, collapses, coma, and paralysing
self-doubt, all of which make identification of him with his author
irresistible.

Nietzsche's characterizations of *TSZ* as by far the most important book
that mankind has been given so far, etc., indicate that however
critically he advised his disciples to take it, self-critique was not in his
line, at least then. All the more upsetting that the publication of the
first three parts was a non-event in the cultural life of Europe, and that
Part IV was brought out privately at Nietzsche's own expense in 1885. It
shows how far removed he was from a close understanding of the
state of his contemporaries that he should have been in the least
surprised. If his previous books had fallen like stones, what could be
made of a work which was more innovative in one way, more archaic in
another, than anything produced by a 'philosopher' since Plotinus?

What must seem astonishing is that Nietzsche's writing went on unabated, but mostly in the mode established by the books that had preceded *TSZ*. He insisted that everything he wrote after *TSZ* was a commentary on it, but that seems to have been more in the nature of an attempt at self-reassurance than a genuine assessment of their nature or quality. For one thing, the *Übermensch* is never heard of again; the Eternal Recurrence rarely recurs; and the Will to Power simmers away alternately on and under the surface. For another, the progress through the first post-Zarathustra book, *Beyond Good and Evil*, through his masterpiece *The Genealogy of Morals*, to the torrential pamphlets of the last year, has little to do with anything stated or adumbrated in *TSZ*.

It strikes me rather that with the writing of *TSZ* Nietzsche got a great deal out of his system in one go – and fortunately so. However indefensible they may have been, the grotesque and earnest parodies of Nietzsche which constituted the cults I referred to in Chapter 1 all took their inspiration from that book – they could not have taken it from any of the others, where the tones of mockery and tentativeness, which continue right up to the end, amid stridencies and denunciations, foreclose on the possibility of doctrine. All Nietzsche's books demand close attention, but to profit from *TSZ* one needs to be flexible and vigilant in a way that few readers, confronted with the orotundities of the opening pages, are likely to be. Without his prophet, there would have been no chance of Nietzsche's sister Elisabeth clothing him in a white robe for exhibition to tourists, after he had reached a state of advanced insanity, as himself 'the transfigured prophet'. Nor would his friend Peter Gast have been able to say, as Nietzsche's body was lowered into the ground, 'May your name be holy to all future generations!' when Nietzsche had written in the last Chapter of *Ecce Homo* 'I have a terrible fear that I shall one day be pronounced *holy*: one will indeed guess why I bring out this book *beforehand* . . . I do not want to be a saint, rather even a buffoon' (*EH*, 'Why I am a Destiny', 1).

His first book after *TSZ* is given a deliberately misleading title: *Beyond Good and Evil*, whatever may be said by Nietzsche or his commentators, suggests a transvaluation of *all* values, and not just a man preparing to replace those we have with a new set, however drastic. It is this that provides what excuse there is (none, if one reads carefully) for thinking that Nietzsche was intent on eliminating value from the world. There is no value to be discovered in the world, but it is therefore all the more imperative to endow it with value. But how is that to be done? We have, Nietzsche insists, always done it, but up until now that is not what we thought we were doing. And the movement from imagining that we are finding what in fact we are inventing, to a full realization that that is what we are doing, has to be negotiated with the utmost combined lightfootedness and caution if we are not to fall headlong into the abyss of nihilism.

The initial movements of thought in *BGE* are cunningly designed to create the maximum sense of unease about where we stand with respect to what we take to be our fundamental value: truth. If he can make us share some of his doubts about what our will to truth comes to, we are putty in Nietzsche's hands, because there is nothing more basic to which we can appeal. It is a typical move of his, to proceed from truth to the will to truth, to psychologize our relations with the world. He puts it in riddling form, as he acknowledges by saying that it is hard to know who is Oedipus here and who the Sphinx. 'We asked rather about the *value* of this will. Suppose we want truth: *why not rather* untruth? and uncertainty? even ignorance?'

It is not only millennia of attachment to an ingrained set of values that makes this so odd. For the sheer idea of wanting, that is knowing that one wants, untruth, has a zany quality about it. It is perfectly acceptable to say that one wants to remain in ignorance of some matter, or is uninterested in what the truth about it may be. We often do. But to say or claim that one wants the untruth about something smacks of a logical paradox. It is a quite different matter from being inertly complacent about the lack of rigour with which one looks for truth, as almost everyone is on all important issues. And it is also different from wanting to believe what is in fact false, though we do not know that. There is nothing odd in saying 'Many of my beliefs are false', which any sane person would agree to. But there is terminal oddness in saying 'Many of my beliefs are false, including the following: . . . 'and then providing a list. For in saying something is false one is saying that one does not believe it.

I am making a meal of this point because Nietzsche does seem to suggest that we can investigate the question of why we have a will to truth, i.e. to assenting to propositions the truth of which we have, or think we have, ascertained. If he does mean that, he is confused. Suppose that he is not, what does he mean? He keeps on (a characteristic ploy) changing the subject at such a rate that we lose grip, if we are not careful, of what he is investigating. So in Section 2 he moves on to a wide range of issues, the most searching of which is the metaphysician's 'faith in opposite values'. He shrewdly points out that metaphysicians, whom he has been attacking since he stopped being one himself in *BT*, though they tend to claim that they doubt everything possible, do not call in question the possibility of deriving something from its opposite. Since, for example, they deny that selflessness could emerge from selfishness, purity of heart from lust, truth from error, they posit 'the lap of Being, the intransitory, the hidden god, the "thing-in-itself" ', since nothing less imposing will do for the source of our values. In other words, ones which Nietzsche does not use here, but often elsewhere, Plato has called the tune. There is falsity, ugliness, and wickedness ('appetite') in the mundane; so their opposites must originate in the supra-mundane.

By contrast, Nietzsche doubts:

> whether there are any opposites at all, and secondly, whether these
> popular valuations and opposite values on which the metaphysicians

put their seal, are not perhaps merely foreground estimates, only provisional perspectives . . . frog perspectives, as it were, to borrow an expression painters use. For all the value that the true, the truthful, the selfless may deserve, it would still be possible that a higher and more fundamental value for life might have to be ascribed to deception, selfishness and lust. It might even be possible that what constitutes the value of these good and revered things is precisely that they are insidiously related, tied to, and involved with the wicked, seemingly opposite things – maybe even one with them in essence. Maybe!

(BGE I. 2)

Speculating at this rate is dangerous, and Nietzsche does not let up. Plodding behind, let us notice to what extent he has already changed his focus from the opening section. For now he is scrutinizing not our will to truth, but our will to think that certain kinds of statement are true, those that contrast things we hold in low esteem with things that we value. What he is doing is giving examples, which he hopes we will find unwelcome but will not be able to counter, of how what we take to be the basic value of truth is in fact derivative from other, more instinctive, values. Truth, we take it, certainly if we are philosophers, is a matter for conscious reflection. But, vaulting on to his next point, Nietzsche puts the greater part of the philosopher's activity on the instinctive level, and claims that the conscious thoughts of philosophers are dictated by their inclinations, 'valuations, or more clearly physiological demands for the preservation of a certain kind of life' (<i>BGE</i> I. 3). This sounds like bad news; but in yet another piece of intellectual demoralization, Nietzsche goes on

> The falseness of a judgement is not for us necessarily an objection to a judgement; in this respect our new language may sound strangest. The question is to what extent it is life-promoting, life-preserving, species-preserving, perhaps even species-cultivating . . . To recognize untruth as a condition of life – that certainly means resisting accustomed value

feelings in a dangerous way; and a philosophy that risks this would by
that token alone place itself beyond good and evil

(BGE I. 4)

Such a philosophy would place itself beyond good and evil by dint of its
denial of the grounds that we give for our value judgements. It would
also, I think it is part of Nietzsche's intention to intimate, make us into
anthropologists of the whole human scene, so that we would be
beyond good and evil in the same way that anthropologists of
primitive tribes are 'beyond' the concepts of the tribes they study. But
this is to place us very high indeed – us new philosophers: *BGE* is
subtitled 'Prelude to a Philosophy of the Future'. Anyone who is
concerned with so far-reaching an enterprise as Nietzsche since he
embarked on his 'Thoughts on the prejudices of morality' in *D* is bound
to feel himself taking up a loftier and loftier position as he realizes that
everything about morality is prejudice, but that does produce acute
problems as to how he is to achieve and then maintain so exalted a
perspective. He is in a way in the reverse position from what is known
as 'the anthropologist's dilemma'. That is of how to understand a tribe
whose concepts one does not share – for understanding is in part a
preparedness to apply the same concepts to the same situations; and if
one's disagreements are as comprehensive as ours with a tribe that
practises witchcraft, based on a set of views about the causal
relationship between formulas and rituals performed by some
members of the tribe, and the resultant state of some other members,
then it looks as if in some way we cannot grasp what is going on – or at
least that has been thought by some anthropologists and theorists of
the subject.

But Nietzsche, in trying to take up an anthropological stance to his
own society, and the central traditions of Western culture, is in a
different but perhaps more worrying plight. For he is the first person to
insist that there is no such thing as a substantial self, which can view
the world with dispassion, uncontaminated by its environment. We

are, he is ever more anxious to point out, nothing over and above our drives, our memories, and the other states and dispositions which grammar (and deriving from grammar, philosophy, and theology) leads us to attribute to a subject, which turns out to be mythical. And these mental states are determined by the society in which we grow up, to a point where we are unable to stand apart from ourselves and take a look at what we would be like if we had independence from what constitutes us. So what enables him to achieve a god's-eye view of the human condition, from which he can make judgements beyond good and evil?

He never answers this question directly, though he is certainly aware of it. His solution, in so far as it is meant to be that, lies in what has become in recent years one of his most celebrated views, thanks to its being so congenial to deconstructionists. He does not believe that there are such things as facts without interpretations, though his strongest claim on that score is to be found in his notebooks (printed as section 481 of *WP*). In his published work, his most explicit statement is 'There is *only* a perspective seeing, only a perspective "knowing" and the *more* affects we allow to speak about one thing, the more complete will our "concept" of this thing, our "objectivity" be' (*GM* III 12). So what interprets and what is interpreted are both in a different position from that which a naïve epistemology would attribute to them. We are bound to see things from our point of view, so it is a good idea to take up as many points of view as possible. We shall never get to 'the things themselves', because of us and also because we have no reason to think that, in the sense that traditionally has been given to that phrase, there are such things.

Nietzsche never worked out his own epistemology in detail, nor is there any reason to think that he would have particularly wanted to. As always, his overriding concern is with culture, and he says what he does about perspectives – not nearly enough to make possible an uncontroversial account of his view – in order to stress that our beliefs, specifically about value, are never free from the place we occupy in the world. If one tried to press his perspectivism harder than that, it would seem very dubious. That is no doubt the reason for the plethora of inverted commas sprouting round tricky words in the quotation above from *GM*. But so far as values are concerned, he demonstrates in his own practice how one can take up various attitudes to a particular problem, never arriving at the truth concerning it, because that would be to suppose that in the world of values there are truths – and thus, also, to give that privileged place to truth that he is keen to dispute.

But there does seem to be one criterion, which makes its debut in his first book, and continues to the end of his work, by which all else is finally judged. That is: life. We have seen him saying in *BGE* that the falseness of a judgement is not necessarily an objection to it, the question being to what extent it is life-promoting, life-preserving. And in the same year as he wrote *BGE* he produced many versions of prefaces to some of his previous books, *BT* included, in which again 'life' is taken to be the measure of all things: 'to look at science in the perspective of the artist, but at art in that of life' is what, in 'An Attempt at Self-Criticism' he says was 'the task this audacious book dared to tackle for the first time.' Life as opposed to what? That is not something that Nietzsche ever gives a clear answer to, any more than other distinguished artists and philosophers have. He is certainly not concerned with the *quantity* of life around – if anything, he would prefer there to be much less, and of a superior order. But what is a superior order of life? Well, the *Übermensch*, one imagines. But we have seen that one has to imagine all too much about the *Übermensch*, that blank cheque which Zarathustra issues without any directions about cashing it, for him to be helpful. Power? Certainly that is heavily involved, since life is Will to Power; but not all power is approved by Nietzsche; it could not be, or he would approve of everything. And power and life are, in his philosophy, two terms that inhabit so much the same conceptual region that rather than one illuminating the

other, they both seem to stand in need of some independent
light.

All the great advocates of life as an ultimate criterion – Christ, Blake,
Nietzsche, Schweitzer, D. H. Lawrence, for a few – have been vigorous
in their condemnation of an enormous amount of it, on behalf of other,
more precious forms or varieties. And in a way one sees what they all
mean, though if bacteria could speak they would no doubt have
claimed every bit as much right to live as the larger organisms in
whose favour Schweitzer was eliminating them. And what the five
people I mentioned counted as being 'on the side of life' or 'life-
denying' varies in many respects sharply. Yet they do not seem to be
saying *nothing* when they speak on behalf of life, vague and often
unhelpful for making decisions as they are. Often what Nietzsche
means is something close to vitality or even liveliness. That becomes
increasingly clear in his judgements on art, where the test is, in the
later and last writings, whether it manifests an overabundance on the
part of its creator, or whether it is the product of need and deprivation.
It is for being an exemplar of the latter that Wagner is condemned, to
take the ubiquitous case.

It is at least clear that vitality is a necessary, if not a sufficient,
condition for Nietzsche's approving of anything in his later work. A
figure such as Goethe (subject to some mythologization by Nietzsche,
naturally) is venerated because of the number of diverse impulses he
was able to organize and mobilize, in the course of a life of almost
unexampled productivity in a wide variety of fields. And yet (to go
back for a moment to style) everything he did bears his stamp. But
there is, lurking just under the surface of Nietzsche's criterion, a strong
and disturbing tension. Henry Staten, whose superb book, already
quoted from at length, is organized round this tension, puts a crucial
part of it tersely:

> On the one hand, there is an overall economy that includes both health

and decay, on the other hand, Nietzsche cannot deny himself the satisfaction of sounding the note of strong ascendancy over the forces of decay. And the question of the relation between these forces is also the question of Nietzsche's identity.

(Staten, 1990: 30)

Which is to say that Nietzsche is drawn to overall affirmation, as the Eternal Recurrence shows, if it shows anything. But the movement of affirmation is powerfully countered by a fastidious revulsion from almost everything he encounters, certainly among his contemporaries. This tension is fairly closely parallel to the one regarding life: all of life, or only the noblest, best, strongest kind?

It is amazing that, so far as I can discover, Nietzsche never noticed this rending cleavage in his work, all the more so in that it must reflect crises that he experienced in trying to cope with his horribly painful life. And it can be seen, too, as an extrapolation from Apollo and Dionysus in *BT*. For Apollo presents life in a way that is tolerable, through exclusion of the chthonic depths; while Dionysus ignores nothing, forcing us to face the fundamental terrors of existence. If Nietzsche had not found himself, for many reasons, having to abandon the artist's metaphysics of *BT*, he would have had set up for himself a system which did justice to the conflicting impulses in his make-up, and an account of why he had them.

But it was not long before 'the terrible', that which we are hardly able to bear, came to have a quite different significance for Nietzsche from that portended in *BT*. In that book it is spectacular, a matter usually of suffering, sometimes of joy, on a primal scale. To affirm it is glamorous as well as almost impossible, except to the greatest tragedians. This is where Nietzsche shows most blatantly his immaturity and lack of experience. But when experiences came along, all too many too soon, it turned out that though some of them were appalling in a way that could, with not too much inflation, be seen under the aegis of

Dionysus, the vast majority were of a kind for which no allowance had been made in *BT*, and which left Nietzsche at a loss: they were trivial, small, no more glamorous than suffering from a large number of insect bites. It turned out that what is hardest to face, at least if you are Nietzsche, is the quotidian, that which it would be an insult to the artistic gods to ascribe to either of them. Hence he is unable to fit the nineteenth-century art form *par excellence*, the realistic novel, into any artistic category. There is, of course, also the novel's antipode, instrumental music, flourishing in a way and on a scale unprecedented in Western culture. But music fulfilled its truest role when it was part of tragedy. Now we have a ghastly split between the mundane, apparently unsusceptible to any form of artistic transfiguration, and 'pure' music whose splendour and misery are that it is uncontaminated by 'reality'. The attempt to bring them together has resulted in the charlatanry of Wagner, the most painful, because most deceptive, of contemporary phenomena. No one else even appears on the horizon to unite what should never have been separated. (Nietzsche's last-minute proclamation of the genius of Bizet in *Carmen* is, given the gravity of the situation, bathetic. Nietzsche needed a work in which significance was pervasive, whereas, as Adorno has argued, *Carmen* uncompromisingly refuses meaning to any event.)

Zarathustra says at one point in Part III, when he temporarily returns to his mountain home for refreshment:

> Down there all speech is vain. There, forgetting and passing by are the best wisdom: *that* I have learned now. He who would grasp everything human would have to grapple with everything. But for that my hands are too clean. I do not even want to inhale their breath; alas, that I lived so long among their noises and vile breath!
>
> (*TSZ* III, 'The Return Home')

And he continues with a horrified account of the empty unavoidable chatter he encountered at ground level. That was, I am sure, Nietzsche's usual reaction to his urban surroundings. But to exclude almost the whole of human life was an odd move for the unqualified affirmer. He tries to duck what he glimpsed, it seems, as an inconsistency in his outlook by talking of 'forgetting and looking away', just as at the opening of Book IV of *GS* he had said '*Looking away* shall be my only negation.' But what if what you have to look away from is so ubiquitous that you either have to live in a cell or leave the world behind and ascend to your mountain cave? That shows a despair more crushing than mixing with banality and denouncing it. And when Nietzsche has that thought, or something like it, he resolves instead that one way or another he will affirm everything. There is, after all, something less than impressive in a philosophy of unlimited yes-saying which begins by ruling most things out of bounds. That is recognized by Zarathustra when he says that the biggest objection to the Eternal Recurrence is the thought that the small man will recur. Nietzsche puts it with his own brand of desperate humour in *EH*, where he writes 'I confess that the deepest objection to the Eternal Recurrence, my real idea from the abyss, is always my mother and my sister' (*EH*, 'Why I am so wise', 3; this passage was suppressed by Elisabeth and only published in the 1960s).

There is, too, a further worry about affirming everything. Although Nietzsche was attracted by formulas such as *amor fati* he was also aware of the nearly inevitable tepidity of them. For there is not an easily specifiable difference between affirmation and resignation – or rather, one can say that their modality differs but it is hard to know in practice what that comes to. Is it a matter of beaming versus shrugging? And is that enough? To affirm life in all its richness, which includes on the comprehensive reading in all its poverty, does not, I take it, involve actually doing any particular things; at most it involves taking up an attitude which welcomes whatever it finds. But if what it overwhelmingly finds is smallness, spiritual squalor, it would seem to be required of the affirmer to intervene and raise the tone of the world. That is the gravamen of Adorno's succinctly expressed objection to Nietzsche (Adorno, 1974: 97–8). It is also what is working away beneath the surface of a great deal of Nietzsche himself, nowhere more acutely than in *BGE*. It means that he has to move on once more, propelled by the aporia presented in one book to resolve it in the next – the characteristic movement that drives him from work to work (see Peter Heller, 1966). But though his next book is his most magnificent, it fails, thanks to Nietzsche's intransigent honesty, to lessen the tension, indeed it screws it up even further, leaving the books of the last year, 1888, to oscillate between unexampled anathemas and furious exaltation.

Chapter 8
Masters and Slaves

Nietzsche subtitled *The Genealogy of Morals* 'A polemic', and the next page announces that it is 'A sequel to my last book, *Beyond Good and Evil*, which it is meant to supplement and clarify'. It is in a different form, at least superficially, from his other works, in that it consists of three titled essays, divided into sometimes quite lengthy sections. It has some of the appurtenances of an academic essay, but that is Nietzsche teasing. It is much better regarded as a send-up of academic procedures, though it is, in its content, a work of extreme seriousness. It is easily Nietzsche's most complex text, at least for the first two essays, performing dialectical reversals at a rate that only just prevents the virtuosic from sliding into the chaotic.

It is worth noting that it was after he heard Eduard Hitschmann read excerpts from *GM* in 1908 that Freud said Nietzsche 'had a more penetrating knowledge of himself than any other man who ever lived or was likely to live' (Jones, 1955: ii. 385). Since *GM* is Nietzsche's most sustained and profound attempt to make sense of suffering, and of how other people have tried to make sense of it, it may not be surprising that Freud, who devoted his life in a radically different way to the same enterprise, should have been stirred to this remarkable compliment. The astounding twists and turns of *GM*, occasionally issuing in downright contradiction, are the result of Nietzsche's constant broodings on the variety of methods which people have developed for coping with it. So (to anticipate one of his lines of thought) the ascetic imposes one kind of suffering on himself in order to escape from many other kinds. By itself that is not to be judged. But when, in the Third Essay, 'What is the Meaning of Ascetic Ideals?', he begins to examine the varieties of asceticism practised by artists, philosophers, priests and their flocks, evaluations proliferate and enter into relationships with one another whose complexity suggests that Nietzsche has reached a point of subtlety, often disguised by the crude vigour of its expression, which admits that the phenomena are no longer susceptible of intelligible ordering.

The movement of the book as a whole is from a simplicity of contrasts which, both in its form and content, induces incredulity, to a collapse of categories which hovers around incomprehensibility. The initial postulate of the First Essay, 'Good and Evil', 'Good and Bad', is of 'the noble', those who are entitled to be legislators of value because of their position, 'who felt and established their actions as good, that is, of the first rank, in contradistinction to all the low, low-minded, common and plebeian. It was out of this *feeling of distance* that they first seized the right to create values and to coin names for values: what had they to do with utility!' (*GM* I. 2) It is here that Nietzsche makes fully explicit another force of the phrase 'beyond good and evil'. For they are now said to be the categories of the slaves, who regard their masters as evil, and define 'good' by what is unlike them. By contrast, the original nobles first define themselves, and then call 'bad' whatever lacks their qualities. Clearly Nietzsche thinks that the latter procedure is superior to the former, which is inherently reactive, a product of negation. The trouble with these proto-nobles is that in the simplicity of their approach to life they are boring. Incorrigibly healthy, indifferent to suffering, uninterested in condemnation of those unlike themselves, they are the creators of value without having any of the materials to work on which make evaluations pointful.

In *BGE* Nietzsche had repeatedly stressed the necessity of vigilant evaluation – life depends on it. But how is it to operate simultaneously with the unrestricted affirmation which sometimes seems to be the only positive value, and which the noble once came closest to? This takes us back, as it should, to the aporia of *BGE*. To live without regrets or nostalgia, for instance, sounds in a way wonderful. And yet how can one not regret wasted time, missed opportunities, failure, as well as happiness of a kind that one can never know again? And how can one avoid, in these regrets, going in for a lot of comparison and contrast, the bases of evaluation? In general, some of Zarathustra's most pregnant words seem to settle the matter:

> And you tell me, my friends, that there is no disputing of taste and tasting? But all of life is a dispute over taste and tasting. Taste – that is at the same time weight and scales and weigher; and woe unto all the living that would live without disputes over weight and scales and weighers!
>
> (*TSZ* II, 'On Those Who are Sublime')

So it is clear that the noble, the original 'masters', are not for Nietzsche an unequivocal subject of praise. Equally, the 'slaves', those who resent the masters, are more likely, in their industrious enquiries into the sources of their misery, to emerge with interesting answers. But the answers become too interesting, and any possibility of heroic simplicity is lost. Since there is no question but that it has been lost, irrecoverably, we late men, decadents, must have the courage of our lateness and pursue the argument wherever it leads. To abbreviate Nietzsche's most searching points in a brutal way (it is hopeless to try to summarize *GM*): the slaves found that by being subtler than their masters (no difficult feat) they could exercise their Will to Power in ways that, though despicable from the noble perspective, were effective; even, finally, to the extent of converting the masters to their own values. That was the inevitable progression from the Jews in captivity to Christianity, the greatest moral coup ever perpetrated. Among many other things, that is what is traced in the Second Essay,

'"Guilt", "Bad Conscience", and the Like'. By condemning worldly values such as pride, prosperity, satisfaction with oneself, and replacing them by modesty, humility, and the rest, Christians succeeded in making their rulers as small as they were. But to do that they cultivated values which contained the seeds of Christianity's own destruction. Nietzsche quotes one of the most persuasive passages in Book V of *GS* near the end of *GM*:

> Christian morality itself, the concept of truthfulness taken more and more strictly, the confessional subtlety of the Christian conscience translated and sublimated into the scientific conscience, into intellectual cleanliness at any price. To view nature as if it were a proof of the goodness and providence of a God; to interpret history to the glory of a divine reason, as the perpetual witness to a moral world order and moral intentions . . . – that now seems to belong to the *past*, that has the conscience *against it* . . .
>
> (*GS* 357)

And he continues *GM* with one of his most stupendous passages:

> All great things bring about their own destruction through an act of self-overcoming: thus the law of life will have it, the law of the necessity of 'self-overcoming' in the nature of, life – the lawgiver himself eventually receives the call: Submit to the law you yourself proposed. In this way Christianity as a dogma was destroyed by its own morality; in the same way Christianity as a morality must now perish too; we stand on the threshold of this event.
>
> (*GM* III 27)

And his very last remarks in this book are about the collapse of morality, hijacked by Christianity, as the will to truth gains self-consciousness.

Note: 'all great things' and then an account of Christianity's self-destruction. *GM* is Nietzsche's most balanced book not by virtue of the sobriety of its style – Nietzsche is no longer interested in that – but by its taking contraries to extremes and giving them all their due, so that he presides over a battle, or rather several, in which he delights in arming both sides as powerfully as possible and lending all the assistance he can to getting them to fight it out. That enables him to indulge in the studied unfairmindedness of his last books. *GM* is both a creative retrospective and a point of departure for his next phase, which was to be abruptly cut off.

This retrospective dimension of the book is what gives the Third Essay, 'What is the Meaning of Ascetic Ideals?', its strange structure, seemingly wandering far from the points he has been making earlier. For in it he conducts a survey of what ascetic ideals mean to various groups of people who have always been important to him, in the light of their self-inflicted sufferings. Life is dreadful anyway; so why make it worse by practising asceticism, the voluntary increase in what one would expect people to avoid? Suffering that is merely contingent, visited on us without explanation, is unendurable. But if we inflict it on ourselves we can understand it, and extend our understanding to the whole of life.

Artists are the first to be scrutinized; but that soon comes down to a consideration (not one of Nietzsche's big surprises) of Wagner, and of what Nietzsche took to be his embracing of chastity in his old age. In the course of it Nietzsche says 'one does best to separate an artist from his work, not taking him as seriously as his work . . . The fact is that if he were it, he would not represent, conceive, and express it: a Homer would not have created an Achilles nor a Goethe a Faust if Homer had been an Achilles or Goethe a Faust' (*GM* III. 4). The conclusion is that the artist is conscienceless, adopting any pose that will further his work. He uses experience for the purpose of creation, which may have little to do with 'the truth'. 'What, then, is the meaning of ascetic ideals? In the case of an artist, as we see, nothing whatever!' (*GM* III. 5). Having at the outset of his career said that 'art is the true metaphysical activity of this life' and then abandoned metaphysics, Nietzsche is by now not disposed to think that there are any intimate relations between art and reality. In a late note he writes: 'For a philosopher to say "the good and the beautiful are one" is infamy; if he goes on to add "also the truth", one ought to thrash him. Truth is ugly. We have art lest we *perish of the truth*' (*WP* 822). And yet he always takes art as the paradigm of human activity. So it seems – a further aporia, not addressed – that artists are inherently suspicious characters, while art is a life-preserving evasion of the truth, often presented – certainly by Wagner – as the truth. Any artist who merely tries to produce a report on reality is roundly condemned. Apart from them, the rest 'have at all times been valets of some morality, philosophy or religion' (*GM* III. 5). So as far as understanding ascetic ideals goes, 'let us eliminate the artists' (ibid.).

Nietzsche next turns to philosophers. To be a philosopher is to practise asceticism for one's own benefit. But here asceticism comes to no more than, in the first place, being single-minded and denying oneself various pleasures for the sake of a single-mindedly pursued goal. Whereas the *compulsion* to asceticism is the result of horror at the possibility of enjoyment of life, because one does not deserve it. There is asceticism chosen and asceticism imposed, and they are utterly separate phenomena. Those who practise it at the behest of priests do not do it to achieve any good for which it is a prerequisite, but because the guilt the priests have made them feel drives them to an increase of suffering which they deserve: the hideous cruelty of explaining to them why life is painful by inflicting more pain on them: they are responsible for their own suffering.

Such a bizarre phenomenon clearly both fascinates and appals Nietzsche, just as he is amazed at people's capacity for turning their backs on the whole thing and dwelling in a state of frivolous misery. 'Man is the sick animal', but it seems that all available remedies have been tried and found wanting. Hence Nietzsche's growing impatience, expressed in the telegraphic prose of his last year, and his longing for total revolution. As his own sufferings became more acute, which they did at an alarming rate during 1887 and 1888, he became less tolerant of any view of things that tried in any way to claim a meaning for them; and that is how he conceives morality during this period, as no more than a collection of frequently terrifyingly adroit moves to persuade people that behaving well and prospering are connected. At the close of *GM* he allows himself the hope that 'there can be no doubt that morality will gradually perish'. But he cannot have believed that. For so much of *GM* has been devoted to showing the infinitely resourceful ways in which the priestly, who need not, of course, be actually in the service of the Church, contrive to keep morality going. And as we become smaller – without Christianity there is the possibility of becoming bigger, but the overwhelming probability that we shall cling to our Christian-based morality, claiming that it only needs a few adjustments to bring the heaven on earth of utilitarianism – we will lose even the capacity to recognize greatness, supposing it were any longer possible. Slave-morality has triumphed. We are content to be slaves even when there are no masters. The brilliant last section of *GM* sums it all up without simplifying or making crude:

> Man, the bravest of animals and the one most accustomed to suffering, does *not* repudiate suffering as such; he *desires* it, he even seeks it out, provided he is shown a meaning for it, *a purpose* of suffering. The meaninglessness of suffering, *not* suffering itself, was the curse that lay over mankind so far – *and the ascetic ideal offered man meaning!* It was the only meaning offered so far; any meaning is better than none at all . . . man was *saved* thereby, he possessed a meaning, he was no longer like a leaf in the wind . . . he could now *will* something; no matter at first to what end, why, with what he willed: *the will itself was saved.*

> We can no longer conceal from ourselves what is expressed by all that willing which has taken its direction from the ascetic ideal: this hatred

of the human, and even more of the animal, and more still of the material, this horror of the senses, of reason itself, this fear of happiness and beauty, this longing to get away from all appearance, change, becoming, death, wishing, from longing itself – all this means – let us dare to grasp it – *a will to nothingness*, an aversion to life, a rebellion against the most fundamental presuppositions of life; but it is and remains a *will!* ... And, to repeat in conclusion what I said at the beginning: man would rather will *nothingness* than *not* will.

(GM III. 28)

With those words Nietzsche ends the last truly original book he was to write. It is extraordinary how exhilarating it is, since it contains almost no messages of hope. But diagnosis carried out at this level strikes one – however illusorily – as being halfway to cure.

Chapter 9

Philosophizing with a Hammer

1888, the last year of Nietzsche's sane life, was very productive, but in an increasingly odd way. What was to have been the most important of his books, *The Transvaluation of All Values*, was begun and abandoned, not, one may suspect, for lack of stamina, but because in the end Nietzsche found himself at a loss. The often-used phrases about the return of innocence, the birth of a new consciousness, and so on, must have seemed to him ever more hollow, if he could not incarnate them in artistic form. So he devoted himself to further polemics, written in a style of hard clarity which even he had never attained before. It is quite wrong to claim, as some commentators have, that he cheapened what he had been saying by reducing it to slogans.

These polemics, though, take on again and again an elegiac ring, as he settles accounts with the great figures who had preoccupied him throughout his life. There are two pamphlets on Wagner, the impact of whom, personal as well as artistic, he had never managed to shake off. The first of them, *The Case of Wagner*, *is* shrewd and hilarious, and its total effect, as its most intelligent commentators, such as Thomas Mann, have pointed out, is of curiously inverted eulogy. Quite a lot of the eulogy is not even inverted. It seems that at the end, when he surveyed his whole range of artistic experience, the work that meant most to him was, as it had been in *BT*, *Tristan und Isolde*. Certainly he never managed anything more eloquent than his account of its effects on him – still. The attack on Wagner as a decadent, portraying in mythic dimensions characters who belong in Flaubert, can all too easily be used for a *tu quoque*: 'Transposed into hugeness, Wagner does not seem to have been interested in any problems except those which now preoccupy the little decadents of Paris. Always five steps from the hospital. All of them entirely modern, entirely *metropolitan* problems. Don't doubt it' (*CW* 9). And Nietzsche? He is surely presiding over proceedings inside the hospital.

The second anti-Wagner polemic, *Nietzsche Contra Wagner*, is a collection of sections from his earlier books, from *HAH* to *BGE*, slightly modified. It is strangely called by Walter Kaufmann 'perhaps Nietzsche's most beautiful book', which is not to say it does not contain beautiful passages, but it is an album rather than an organized work and is anyway only twenty pages long. As much as anything else, it is part of Nietzsche's self-mythologization, in which he represents himself as 'being condemned to Germans', with Wagner providing an apparent contrast with the rest of them, until he too 'suddenly sank down, helpless and broken, before the Christian cross' (*NCW*, 'How I broke away from Wagner', 1). He portrays Wagner as the great antipode to himself, what he might have become if he had not had the strength to realize what dangers were involved in being a fully-fledged Romantic. The density of insight into music, Wagnerian music-drama, the nature of Wagner's genius, is flabbergasting, and the gathering together of these passages adds to their impact. But more than anything it is testimony to the abiding love of Nietzsche for forbidden things.

That could be claimed as even more true of *The Antichrist*, which, in the centre of its strident but effective polemics, gives a portrayal of Christ as the 'great symbolist, [in that he] accepted only *inner* realities as realities, as "truths" – that he understood the rest, everything natural, temporal, spatial, historical, only as signs, as occasions for parables' (*A* 34). This passage, as it continues, reaches heights of ecstatic lyricism which make one wonder how Nietzsche is going to be able to beat a retreat. He contrives it via an attack on Christendom of which Kierkegaard might have been proud, and another on St Paul from which he would have vehemently dissented. But Nietzsche's outrage at what the priests have made of Christ's teachings is glorious in its passion, its expression of his nausea at corruption. And he revealingly says: 'only Christian *practice*, a life such as he *lived* who died on the cross, is Christian. Such a life is still possible today, for certain people even necessary: genuine, original Christianity will be possible at all times' (*A* 39). But not for strong spirits, because it depends on faith. 'Faith makes blessed: consequently it lies' (*A* 50). This is from the inveterately puritan Nietzsche, the man who thinks that 'the greatest suspicion of a "truth" should arise when feelings of pleasure enter the discussion of the question "What is true?"' (*A* 50). One might agree, though Nietzsche seems to be putting into abeyance his questioning of the will to truth. And earlier in the same book, in the middle of a devastating attack on Kant's ethics, he writes 'An action demanded by the instinct of life is proved to be *right* by the pleasure that accompanies it; yet this nihilist [Kant] with his Christian dogmatic entrails considered pleasure an *objection*. What could destroy us more quickly than working, thinking, and feeling without any inner necessity, without any deeply personal choice, without *pleasure* – as an automaton of "duty"?' (*A* 11). Though there is not a straightforward contradiction here, there is that characteristic tension between Nietzsche the man who is determined to face everything and not flinch, and Nietzsche the high-flying hedonist.

The most lively, witty, and altogether exhilarating product of 1888 is *Twilight of the Idols*, the title a parody of Wagner's doom-laden *Twilight of the Gods*. It manifests the freedom of complete mastery, though it was written on the very verge of collapse. And it contains Nietzsche's longest, most ardent paeon to Goethe, who had more and more, as Nietzsche gave up on the *Übermensch*, become the prototype of the 'higher man', a concept which gratefully yields examples; while

Zarathustra was insistent that 'there has never yet been an *Übermensch*'. But though every specimen of higher manhood has some reservations entered about him, at least we are able to grasp what Nietzsche is celebrating. So what Goethe 'wanted was *totality*; he fought the mutual extraneousness of reason, senses, feeling and will (preached with the most abhorrent scholasticism by *Kant*, the antipode of Goethe); he disciplined himself to wholeness, he *created* himself' (*TI* 'Skirmishes of an Untimely Man', 49). Nietzsche awards him the highest of all his honours: 'Such a spirit who has *become free* stands amidst the cosmos with a joyous and trusting fatalism, in the *faith* that only the particular is loathsome, and that all is redeemed in the whole – *he does not negate any more*. Such a faith, however, is the highest of all possible faiths: I have baptized it with the name of *Dionysus*' (ibid.). There are striking departures here – we have never before heard from Nietzsche that 'only the particular is loathsome', and wonder what to make of it. But we have heard a great deal, though to very different effect, about Dionysus, never wholly absent from Nietzsche's pantheon, but now making a major come-back in this last year. As always, he is the god of unlimited affirmation. But the context in which he affirms has changed so that the kind of affirmation required is one with little in common with *BT*.

And this is Nietzsche bravely talking about the joys of heaven from a position in hell – for this last year he says No as never before. One might even say that *his* affirmations are only, and this is his tragedy, the negations of negations. His faith – and it is remarkable to find him talking of faith at all in a positive way – is that it is possible to be someone who does not need to negate first. But he could never be that person, and the more dialectical cartwheels he turns, with wonderful and entrancing dexterity, the further he is removed from that ideal. The only Dionysus we can identify him with is the one torn into innumerable agonized fragments.

Postlude
Nietzsche and Life Insurance

1

I suppose that anyone who spends a lot of time in Nietzsche's company, and treats his writings not simply as 'texts' to be elucidated but as experiments in living, which the reader is invited to participate in, must sometimes have a feeling of revulsion, alternating with the excitement and gratitude one feels for the abundance of his insights and the freshness of his approaches to so many well-worn subjects. I hope the earlier chapters of this book have made clear something of the warmth of my response to Nietzsche, because I now wish to register some of the reactions that he evokes in me when I am in a more sceptical phase. Primarily what I shall be doing is enlarging on some points that I have already hinted at, but which seem to me at the moment to carry more weight than I have sometimes felt, or than I shall no doubt feel again. Since, as we saw, he or his spokesman Zarathustra is intent on having the most disagreeing disciples, I shall oblige by raising some fundamental questions about his procedures and his views, questions which are often elementary but which should not on that account be suppressed. Both the methodological and the substantive questions arise from a sense that, whatever he professes, Nietzsche is a writer who is determined not only not to be trumped but not to be trumpable, so that an earnest student sooner or later comes to feel – as in reading Wittgenstein – that he is constantly being set up as a fall guy.

Nietzsche's most frequently used device for rendering himself invulnerable – the state, I shall be arguing, that he is most attracted to, though I have no doubt that he would deny it furiously – is to claim that he is not being categorical about anything, despite strident appearances to the contrary. He is an explorer and experimenter, intent only on setting an example of how, to use a phrase from *GS* 338, 'to find one's own way', something so hard that the advocates of the religion of pity are always interfering with other people so as to avoid the most arduous issues about their own lives. Since Nietzsche is only interested in those people who are candidates for greatness, he necessarily commits himself to a certain extreme of individualism. This means that one can only be a candidate for greatness if one defines oneself, among other ways, in contrast to other people. So, willy-nilly, one will always be bearing others in mind, which is the price that any individualist, at any rate in a late stage of his culture, will have to pay. It is certainly a price that Nietzsche has to pay, as his tirades against his contemporaries make tirelessly clear. He likes to give an impression of lofty indifference to others; yet he is far too fascinated by the varieties of decadence they manifest not to examine them, none too scrupulously, and to point out that 'we others' are not like that.

What I am arguing is that Nietzsche seems to think that his methodology of tentativeness and non-dogmatism, as well as the all-important claim that 'I am not bigoted enough for a system, and not even for *my* system', involves him in a kind of autonomy of outlook as well as of basis. Yet I see no reason why someone should not think that it is up to him to work out the basis of his ethical views, and conclude that the best thing for him is to model himself on some other person. Unless one holds *a priori* that to be oneself is to be radically different from anyone else, there is no conflict, not even an incipient one, in being an individualist and thinking that the best thing one can do is take some other figure for a role model. The degree of Nietzsche's aestheticization of morality will always be disputable, but one respect in which it does seem harmful is the idea that, just as works of art are now required to be original in some sense stronger than that of being discriminable from others, so persons have a similar ethical requirement made on them. As I pointed out in Chapter 5, the relationship between works of art, at any rate in our culture, is quite different from that between persons. Nietzsche seems to think that a collection of extremely similar people would be as boring and superfluous as one of extremely similar works of art. If you take a kind of god's-eye view of the world, which is something that Nietzsche sometimes affects to do, the result may be that you are wearied by 'mass man'; and if people are nearly all too alike then anyone might get tired of them – and up to a point it may well be the case that people who cultivate a uniformity of outlook are tedious. But one hardly needs to go from that to the extreme of demanding that everyone has the highest possible profile. By definition, greatness is a rare quality. That does not mean that most people should be despised or regarded as eliminable for not possessing or aspiring to it.

One reason that Nietzsche is so strenuous about being a non-converter is that in urging us to become who we are he is not committing himself to any ideal which needs to be explored and defended. Yet the terms in which he praises – terms which he tries to keep purely formal – are ones which enable us to pick out certain individuals because they exhibit the properties which those terms name. 'Self-overcoming', for instance, is quite a 'thick' term: we can say that Goethe overcame himself because we know that without his interests he might easily have been no more than the sum of his parts, and gradually would have lost his impressiveness even in them; instead of which he was an astonishingly impressive whole, which is why Nietzsche is so impressed by him in his later writings, taking him as an exemplar, someone who should be imitated for his inimitability.

So Nietzsche's self-alleged refusal to give us any specific advice other than to become ourselves – and no-one will criticize that for being too specific – should not conceal the fact that he is much more categorical than he portrays himself as being. That he frequently changes the positions about which he seems confident should not make us indulge the claims he makes to being tentative. I suspect that he was constitutionally incapable of 'resting in uncertainties', that he did not in any measure possess the poetic temperament as it is delineated by Keats. His flexibilities came from the readiness with which he was prepared to change his mind. When he says he is not bigoted enough for any system, what he should say is that he is not bigoted enough to stick to a system. Not, of course, that at any point he elaborates a system – he was too impatient to do that. Or perhaps it depends what you mean by a system. If you mean that you want all the beliefs you hold to be consistent, then that is an elementary requirement of not succumbing to conceptual chaos. If you mean something more than that, it is incumbent to say what, and Nietzsche does not, apart from expressing his distaste for transcendent metaphysics.

The extreme non-linearity of most of Nietzsche's writing has many appeals, not least that it enables one to follow with a good conscience his advice to dip into *Daybreak* – and so most of his other books – where one feels like it; and lets one off the arduousness of following long stretches of abstract argumentation. It carries, as any conscientious and fascinated reader knows, its own perils. There is the extraordinary phenomenon of the way that individual passages strike one with the utmost force, only to slip the mind a short time after, most often because they have been succeeded by another equally striking, and, one takes it, memorable passage on quite a different topic. That kind of non-systematicness doesn't amount to much more than a lack of organization, not surprising in a mind as fertile as Nietzsche's, so responsive to his experience and other people's reactions to theirs that he is bursting with brilliant things to say on a range of topics larger than almost any philosopher has ever commanded, especially if you take into account the standard that Nietzsche often keeps up for many pages on end. Such torrents of eloquence wedded to insight mean that you feel the need to begin reading the books especially of his middle period as soon as you have finished them, ashamed of your lack of capacity to absorb and remember. It is a process which never ends, and for that there is a lot to be grateful. Even so, it should not be dignified as a principled refusal to be systematic when it is simply what came most naturally to him – compare any of the *Untimely Meditations* with *Human, All Too Human* and you see the immense improvement as soon as he gave up the attempt to write consecutive prose for the length of an essay, let alone a book. Whether or not it was a strategy of defence, it has the effect of one. The question of how to cope with Nietzsche has not yet, so far as I know, been convincingly answered. Read any book or article about him, and notice how the concentration is always on a very few of his remarks, despite the immense number and profound interest of these. Characteristically – and this applies to my own work, of course – selected discussable passages are dealt with, perhaps ones that are in fashion for a few years, just as one or another of Nietzsche's books tends to be at any one time; while the overwhelming proportion of his writing never gets any treatment at all. So Nietzsche is the loser as well as the apparent winner in this particular tactic. He wants us to incorporate his aphorisms into our lives, yet also claims to want us to approach him with unyielding scepticism. Really to live one of his profound aphorisms would take a lot of one's life – how could one do that and yet remain at the distance scepticism requires? Clearly one could not. And in fact anyone who writes as Nietzsche does asks a great deal of trust from his readers, although he pretends that he is asking nothing at all in that line.

I see that my criticisms of his method have moved to being more sympathetic than I expected, another characteristic effect that the always disconcerting Nietzsche has on his readers.

Now to a brief reconsideration of some of Nietzsche's cardinal positions, as I take them to be, and a firmer emphasis on the way in which they serve to protect him from life's contingencies and surprises – the last thing that he should want to be invulnerable to. Yet his most puzzling views – what they amount to and why he held them – often become less puzzling if one accepts that Nietzsche's ambition was to achieve a relationship with the world and his experience of it such that nothing could upset, appal, nauseate, or wound him. It is so difficult to achieve this relationship that if one were to then one would thereby become great. The acuteness of the issue can perhaps be made most clear by considering once more Nietzsche's attitude to pity. Pity is, for him, often a mere symptom of a condition which is deeper and more deplorable than it appears: letting oneself be so affected by suffering, whoever's it may be, that one attempts to mitigate it instead of realizing that it is so ubiquitous that trying to *relieve* it is just silly. One should try to attain a different attitude towards life, which would make pity pointless. Nietzsche never spells his position out with this degree of directness, probably because he is so upset by the proximity of suffering that he commits the meta-sin of being obsessed with considering pity. If pitying people and acting on that is fundamentally a waste of time and effort, then so, after a point – a point which Nietzsche unquestionably passes – is going on about that fact, to such an incorrigible audience. The thing to do is to move to a level where pitying will not arise as a concern, and to display that one has done that, setting the kind of example which even Nietzsche might not object to.

From what perspective could one hope to do that? That is, one could say, Nietzsche's whole concern in the books of his high maturity, before the final period. In fact the section of *GS* which immediately precedes his most celebrated analysis of pity and its effects is the one where he makes clear what his ambition is, albeit in an embryonic way; and also reveals, though unwittingly, how hopeless the ideal that he delineates is. I will quote only part of it – even a fragment of Nietzsche at his most rhetorically brilliant can still have a stunning effect:

> Anyone who manages to experience the history of humanity as *his own history* will feel in an enormously generalised way all the grief of an invalid who thinks of health, of an old man who thinks of the dreams of his youth, of a lover deprived of his beloved, of the martyr whose ideal is perishing ... But if one endured, if one *could* endure this immense sum of grief of all kinds ... if one could burden one's soul with all of this – the oldest, the newest, losses, hopes, conquests, and the victories of humanity; if one could finally contain all this in one soul and crowd it into a single feeling – this would surely have to result in a happiness that humanity has not known so far: the happiness of a god full of power and love, full of tears and laughter, a happiness that, like the sun in the evening, continually bestows its inexhaustible riches, pouring them into the sea, feeling richest, as the sun does, only when even the poorest fisherman is still rowing with golden oars! This godlike feeling would then be called – humaneness.

(GS 337)

In the face of such moving eloquence it seems more than usually petty to scrutinize details. It is a masterstroke of Nietzsche's to put this passage, which certainly gives a drastically new account of 'humaneness', immediately before his attack on old accounts, which relates it to an overriding concern either to avoid or to ameliorate suffering. If one comprehensively lives out the alternative to the life of pity, this 'new humaneness' is what one will achieve. Does it make sense, though, to postulate even the possibility of so exalted a state? To experience *all* is somehow, as throughout his writing life, if not easier then in a way more tolerable than experiencing a selected set of 'losses, hopes, conquests and the victories of humanity'. Despite his loathing and contempt for 'the unconditional', Nietzsche was addicted to a related concept, that of the all-embracing. If one could bear most things, that would mean there were some that maybe one could not – an understandable state. To be 'godlike', or a tragic philosopher or person, one must bear everything; and although it is hard to give sense to such an idea, Nietzsche thinks he knows that it would 'result in a happiness that humanity has not known so far'. Is it not clear that humanity, or even *Übermenschheit*, never will or could know it, since it is not even what Kant would call a 'regulative ideal'? It is, rather, Nietzsche getting drunk with his inimitable capacity to paint in words of the utmost lyricism and poignancy the only states which would make life supportable, but which all turn out to be products of the poet abandoning the exigent requirements of the philosopher.

One more thing is worth noticing, callously, about this passage. One of the things which makes a contrast between pity, the promiscuity of feeling which Nietzsche loathes so vehemently, and this new humaneness, is that in this latter state one is simply adopting an attitude; there is no indication that one would do anything in particular. If we feel with some particular distressed person, we 'assume the role of fate', ignoring the 'whole inner sequence and intricacies that are distress for *me* or for *you*'. If, on the other hand, one goes in for the grand, indeed cosmic, scale of feeling with everything, that leads to nothing in the way of action. There is, indeed, envisageable action which would correspond to Nietzsche's desired state, and for all the astounding energy of his prose, it seems to me at the moment that Nietzsche was not enthused by the idea of acting, only by that of writing, which no doubt is part of the explanation of why his prose is so energetic. Once more, what are the rest of us supposed to do with what energies we can muster?

It would be tedious and depressing to go through the central texts of Nietzsche's affirmation and show that they manifest a similar degree of non-specificity and eagerness to deal with everything simultaneously, which means, in each case, that one has no idea what to do *now*, or why one should do anything rather than anything else. We cannot fail to be struck, once more, with the paradox of Nietzsche's extreme fastidiousness consorting with the will to deny nothing, so that Zarathustra's claim that 'all of life is a dispute over taste and tasting' is contradicted, surely, by the insistence that we affirm it all. And as one cultivates one's attitude of joyful yes-saying, does one tell oneself lies or is 'transfiguring' the past something other than that? As every 'thus it was' becomes a 'thus I willed it', is that a piece of self-deception or something more sublime? Commentators, with a few laudable exceptions, tend not to ask these questions, as if they were themselves offences against good taste.

The passage from *GS* about giving style to one's life raises the same issues. Actually there is the suggestion there that one acts, as when Nietzsche speaks of 'long practice and daily work at it'; though once more it is revising attitudes that seem more important: 'Here the ugly that could not be removed is concealed; there it has been reinterpreted and made sublime'. Yet when we remember that it is one's character that is under consideration, what is this 'reinterpretation' but telling oneself lies? Supposing I said something to someone in order to humiliate them, and find this distasteful and shaming when I remember it. Do I tell myself that I had an alternative motive? Can I always convince myself that I am a beautiful person? Does it minister to the improvement of my character to do so? When Nietzsche says nine sections later, in a characteristic phrase, that 'we want to be the poets of our lives', we recall that in his next book he says, in his Zarathustra persona, 'the poets lie too much, but alas, Zarathustra too is a poet'.

And so – it seems to me – he goes on. He always remains a monist of a certain kind: in *BT* he believed in the Primal One that underlay Apollonian appearance. After ceasing to believe in the possibility of any kind of metaphysical system he remained dismayed by the horror of existence, but all his recipes consist of insisting that existence should be seen under *one* aspect. Why should that make things better, easier, or whatever it is that he wants them to be? Yet another talismanic section is *GS* 276, so beautiful, once more, that it charms one out of thought. This is the passage about not wanting anything to be different, about turning away being his only negation. And that is nothing more than an adumbration of what became his favourite notions, *amor fati* and the Eternal Recurrence, the first of which is the formula for embracing whatever life offers, the second constituting the reason why one had better do that.

In *The Will to Power*, which I remain in general opposed to using, but cannot deny contains many illuminating passages, Nietzsche says, 'Ethics: or "philosophy of desirability." – "Things ought to be different," "Things *shall* be different": dissatisfaction would then be the germ of ethics'.

> One could rescue oneself from it, firstly by selecting states in which one did not have this feeling; secondly by grasping the presumption and stupidity of it: for to desire that something should be different from what it is means to desire that everything should be different – it involves a condemnatory critique of the whole. But life itself is such a desire!
>
> (*WP* 333)

That is characteristic of Nietzsche being genuinely brilliant. It is also characteristically paradoxical. If, as Staten says, life is the desire that things should be different, then so is Nietzsche's life – and to judge from all the evidence it most certainly was. While *amor fati* is his motto, *his* fate was to rail passionately against fate, or the way things are. Can he allow himself that? To judge from Section 11 of the Sleep-walker's Song, quoted earlier, he cannot. To say yes to one single joy is to say yes to everything; but once more we see Nietzsche the consummate lyricist gaining the upper hand – the lyricist in service to the man who believes that if you see the whole of existence as a unity, then you will affirm it all, or at least are committed to affirming it all if you affirm one single part of it. But the fact that everything is 'entangled, ensnared, enamoured' does not mean that one likes it that way. If life *is* the desire that things should be different – and that is certainly a large part of life, indeed the motive that people have for most of what they do – then it is inevitable that one should will to effect some of those differences. As Nietzsche says in a similar but crucially different passage from *BGE* 9, 'Living – is that not precisely wanting to be other than this nature? Is not living – estimating, preferring, being unjust, being limited, wanting to be different? And supposing your imperative "live according to nature" meant at bottom "live according to life", how could you *not* do that? Why make a principle of what you yourselves are and must be?' But if you must be what you are, there is no point in making a *principle* of *anything*, including *amor fati*. Nietzsche gives no indications of how what one might call his stoicism of affirmation is not to collapse into what he elsewhere contemptuously refers to as 'resignationism'.

My claim that Nietzsche is trying to render himself invulnerable is implicit in what I've been saying. Surprisingly, for someone who had as another of his slogans 'Live dangerously!', he seems not to want to be taken by surprise, to be prepared for any contingency, as it were, by claiming that it is necessary, therefore no contingency at all. *Whatever* happens, he wills it; at his most spectacularly paradoxical, he claims that whatever *did* happen, he willed it. Writing at the level of generality that he does, he does not have to deal with cases where it seems not so much superhuman as inhuman to claim that one willed that it should have been so. He thinks, by announcing the most far-reaching doctrines of cosmological necessity, and then claiming infinite repeatability for what they dictate, that he has demonstrated that there never will be and never could be anything new, under or including the sun. Yet at a microscopic level he remains more acute than anyone else – so acute that he has to move to the other extreme – to those 'heights' that he is so keen on. He is prepared to be extraordinarily careful and thorough in explaining how dreadful things – including especially people – are. And as long as he remains at the level of things and people the paralysing horror continues to grow. So when he affirms, it cannot be by selecting approved items, for they are all 'ensnared' in what he detests. He has to take all the phenomena which he loathes, achieve a 'pathos of distance' from them, look down on them; and then he is at last able, thanks to blurred vision, to say yes to everything. In doing that, he betrays all that he actually values, by pretending that he does not value one thing more than another. Sublimity of this kind is indistinguishable from insensibility.

References

Adorno, Theodor (1974), *Minima Moralia* (NLB, London).

Aschheim, Steven E. (1992), *The Nietzsche Legacy in Germany 1890–1990* (University of California Press, Berkeley and Los Angeles).

Bridgwater, Patrick (1972), *Nietzsche in Anglosaxony* (Leicester University Press, Leicester).

Heller, Erich (1988), *The Importance of Nietzsche* (University of Chicago Press, Chicago).

Heller, Peter (1966), *Dialectics and Nihilism* (The University of Massachusetts Press, Amherst, Mass.).

Jones, Ernest (1955), *Siegmund Freud, Life and Work,* ii (Hogarth Press, London).

Kaufmann, Walter (1974), *Nietzsche* (4th edn., Princeton University Press, Princeton, NJ).

Kundera, Milan (1984), *The Unbearable Lightness of Being* (Faber and Faber, London).

Love, Frederick R. (1963), *Young Nietzsche and the Wagnerian Experience* (University of North Carolina Press, Chapel Hill, NC).

Middleton, Christopher (1969) (ed. and trans.), *Selected Letters of Friedrich Nietzsche* (University of Chicago Press, Chicago).

Nehamas, Alexander (1985), *Nietzsche: Life as Literature* (Harvard University Press, Cambridge, Mass.).

Schutte, Ofelia (1984), *Beyond Nihilism: Nietzsche without Masks* (University of Chicago Press, Chicago).

Silk, M. S. and Stern, J. P. (1981), *Nietzsche on Tragedy* (Cambridge University Press, Cambridge).

Solomon, Robert C. and Higgins, Kathleen M. (1988) (eds.), *Reading Nietzsche* (Oxford University Press, New York).

Staten, Henry (1990), *Nietzsche's Voice* (Cornell University Press, Ithaca, NY).

Thompson, Judith J. and Dworkin, Gerald (1968) (eds.), *Ethics* (Harper and Row, Cambridge, Mass.).

Young, Julian (1992), *Nietzsche's Philosophy of Art* (Cambridge University Press, Cambridge).

Further Reading

The amount of writing on Nietzsche in English alone is now growing at
a rate that is both a tribute and a threat. The most magisterial book on
him, by someone deeply sympathetic yet firmly critical, is Erich Heller's
The Importance of Nietzsche (University of Chicago Press, Chicago,
1988). A book somewhat similar in tone, but following patiently
through Nietzsche's development, is F. A. Lea's *The Tragic Philosopher*
(Athlone Press, London, 1993). Originally published in 1957, it is a trail-
blazing work, written, like Heller's and unlike almost everyone else's,
with notable grace and a Nietzschean passion. Unfortunately Lea uses
old and discredited translations for quotation; and he ends surprisingly
by finding that Nietzsche rediscovered the teachings of Christ *and* Paul
for our time. Walter Kaufmann's ill-organized transformation of
Nietzsche into a liberal humanist has its place in the history of
Nietzsche reception *(Nietzsche* 4th edn, Princeton University Press,
Princeton, NJ, 1974).

Of more recent works, the most acclaimed, often setting new
standards in detailed analytic working-through of Nietzsche's
positions, is Alexander Nehamas's *Nietzsche: Life as Literature* (Harvard
University Press, Cambridge, Mass., 1985). It is a demanding but
rewarding book, but Nehamas relies too heavily on unpublished
notebooks of Nietzsche's. More impressive still, as I have indicated in
the text, is Henry Staten's *Nietzsche's Voice* (Cornell University Press,
Ithaca, NY, 1990), a moving and profound series of meditations on

some basic themes in Nietzsche. A less demanding and more critical work on an aspect of Nietzsche which has received little in the way of book-length attention is Julian Young's *Nietzsche's Philosophy of Art* (Cambridge University Press, Cambridge, 1992). Young finds a lot to be indignant about, but his criticisms, in their downrightness, are thought-provoking. A full-length book on *BT* by M. S. Silk and J. P. Stern is *Nietzsche on Tragedy* (Cambridge University Press, Cambridge, 1981), which leaves no stone unturned, so far as the biographical background, the accuracy of Nietzsche's account of Ancient Greece, and so on, are concerned. The essence of the work itself, and the source of its fascination, eludes them, but this is a mine of absorbing information. Nietzsche's politics, or rather his seeming lack of them, are dealt with at length in two overlong but intermittently helpful books, both rather badly written. Tracy Strong's *Friedrich Nietzsche and the Politics of Transfiguration* (expanded edn, University of California Press, Berkeley and Los Angeles, 1988) ranges very widely, and contains a particularly bizarre account of the Eternal Recurrence. Mark Warren's *Nietzsche and Political Thought* (MIT Press, Cambridge, Mass., 1988) distinguishes between what Nietzsche's political views, never presented systematically, were, and what they should have been, from the standpoint of the Frankfurt School of Critical Theory.

There are many collections of essays by various commentators: one that has some excellent contributions to the reading of particular books is *Reading Nietzsche*, edited by Robert C. Solomon and Kathleen M. Higgins (Oxford University Press, 1988). The way that Nietzsche tends to be read in France now is usefully illustrated in a book of translations of Derrida, Klossowski, Deleuze, and so on: *The New Nietzsche*, edited by David B. Allison (Delta, 1977). I find Gilles Deleuze's celebrated *Nietzsche and Philosophy* (trans. Hugh Tomlinson, Athlone Press, London, 1983) quite wild about Nietzsche, but interesting about Deleuze. Many people swear by it. And we are in for an invasion of works from France, where Nietzsche has been idiosyncratically cultivated since World War II.

A Note on Translations

All decent translations of Nietzsche into English or American date from after 1945. Walter Kaufmann was the pioneer of excellence, and his translations of *BT* and everything from *GS* onwards are classics, though his commentaries are obtrusive, self-referential, and lacking insight. R. J. Hollingdale has translated for Penguin and Cambridge University Press the books that Kaufmann did not, and several that he did. They are also serviceable. Introductions to the Penguin series are by me. Kaufmann and Hollingdale joined forces to translate *WP*, which anyone interested in Nietzsche will want to read, and find out for themselves what Nietzsche did not publish, but might or might not have. There is a translation by Douglas Smith of *GM* in Oxford World's Classics.

Index

Visit the
VERY SHORT
INTRODUCTIONS
Web site

www.oup.co.uk/vsi

➤ **Information** about all published titles

➤ News of **forthcoming books**

➤ **Extracts** from the books, including titles
not yet published

➤ **Reviews** and views

➤ **Links** to other **web sites** and main
OUP web page

➤ Information about **VSIs in translation**

➤ **Contact** the editors

➤ **Order** other **VSIs** on-line